AF687954

Contents

Rules are Your Boss

Sarah navigated the market for years - seeing booms, busts, and everything in between. A recent downturn struck hard, causing panic among traders. How did Sarah weather the storm with minimal damage? Her secret weapon was one many underestimates: Self-discipline.

See, being your own boss in the trading world is a double-edged sword. No deadlines, no dress code... sounds awesome until you realize YOU become both the best and worst employee you've ever had. Temptations are everywhere, from chucking strategies mid-downturn to risking big out of impatience. The most successful traders? They write their own rulebook to safeguard against that chaos.

Your Trading Code: Ditch the Corporate Handbook

This personalized trading "code" defines your principles and keeps you on track during those moments when everyone else starts acting crazy. Let's look at the common battlefields these codes take aim at:

- **No More Crazy Risks:** You set ironclad limits on what you'll lose per trade AND for your overall account.
- **Plans Before Profits:** Forget jumping in just because a stock's trending - define your ideal

setup, the exit strategy, AND when it's smarter to do nothing.

- **Mastering the Emotions:** Fear sells at the bottom; greed buys at the top. Code rules keep those wild urges under control.
- **Learning Never Stops:** You schedule knowledge building into your plan - news, analysis, anything relevant to your trades.

Read It, Say It, LIVE It

Write your code like it's the cheesiest motivational wall art, but you know what? That works! Print it, frame it near your trading space... heck, wear it on a t-shirt if you must. Before every trading day, read it aloud - not just the words, but the WHY behind those rules. This programs your brain for success.

Here's the tough part: breaking your code needs a consequence. Not losing your car keys or anything, but maybe you skip trading for a day. Shows those rules have "teeth".

Trading Discipline IRL - Sarah's Case Study

The recent crash hammered portfolios, but thanks to her code, Sarah dodged the worst of it. Her rules forced her to stick to the strategy, even when doubt crept in. Smaller losses kept her capital safe, her mental game solid... meaning she was ready to take advantage when the market bounced back.

Why Bother With All This Strictness?

Because disciplined trading leads to:

- **Death to Dumb Mistakes**: When your rules are clear, trading "on a whim" disappears. Those costly moments just never happen.
- **Forming Good Habits Lightning Fast**: You literally force yourself to do the right things even when they feel hard, until those actions become instinctive.
- **Losses That Teach, Not Traumatize**: When you follow your system, setbacks feel less like failure, more like a learning opportunity to analyze.
- **Confidence You Can't Buy**: Having YOUR playbook and the grit to stick with it creates unshakeable confidence. No guru could give you that.

Building a Code Tailored to YOU

Don't copy someone else's examples! Here's what a strong code includes, plus ideas to get you started:

- **Typical Rulebook Stuff**: "My max loss per trade is 2% of my account". "I trade trend reversals on these timeframes..." etc.
- **Your Personal Weaknesses**: Prone to revenge trading after a bad loss? Add a rule against doubling down. Impatience your issue? Have a strict "walk away" rule.

- **Mistakes We ALL Make:** You accidentally put in a 10x too big order - bam, exit that trade instantly, even if it hurts short-term (beats a HUGE loss later!)

Code Evolution: Keep It Sharp

This isn't some old document you file away! As your skills change, as the market shifts, revisit and update those rules. Your trading code is like your financial shield - make sure it covers every new threat you face along the way.

Examples of Powerful Principles

Here are a few examples of principles bolstering a trader's code. Notice that these aren't generic - they should reflect your unique approach:

- **Risk Management:** "I will never risk more than 2% of my account on a single trade."
- **Trading Methodology:** "I will trade primarily with trend-following systems and focus on confirmed reversals."
- **Emotional Control:** "If I experience three consecutive losses, I will take a break and review my strategy before trading again."
- **Continuing Education:** "I will dedicate 30 minutes each morning to analyzing market news and relevant reports."

Personalizing Your Code: A Few Ideas

These are additional possibilities to tailor your code further:

- **The 'Whoops' Rule:** "If I accidentally execute a trade too large due to misreading data, I will immediately exit the position regardless of short-term loss." (Avoids a minor error spiraling out of control).
- **The 'Anti-Hype' Rule:** "I will not deviate from my strategy based on news sensationalism or social media noise." (Helps filter out distractions).
- **The 'Walk Away' Rule:** "If my preset conditions are not met for a trade, I will not force an entry even if I feel impatient." (Combats boredom-induced errors).

Important! Consider your trading personality when setting rules. If you're prone to revenge trading after a loss, build in a rule against doubling down or immediate re-entry.

Identifying Your Edge

Unleash Your Inner Trading Warrior: Find Your Edge, Dominate the Market

Bruce Lee didn't achieve legendary status by being average. He honed his skills with laser-like intensity until they became extensions of himself. Traders operate in a similarly fierce arena: victory goes NOT to the average, but the focused. Just like a warrior with pinpoint mastery of their weapon, your unique trading edge cuts through the chaos.

Imagine that trader who stays icy while everyone else panics. Bad news hits, markets tank, and most get slaughtered. Yet, their discipline lets them see undervalued gems amid the fear, or stick to their plan for profitable exits before it all crashes down harder. THAT's what trading edges are made of.

What's YOUR Trading Weapon?

Your edge - that combination of skills, gut instincts, and strategies that let you routinely beat the average Joe Trader. It might be:

- **Chart Ninja:** You see patterns forming before others even know to look. Indicators aren't mere tools, they whisper market secrets, giving you an early warning (and often early entry) when everyone else scrambles to react.

- **Market Oracle:** Call it intuition, call it pattern experience, but you sense shifts before they play out. Your entries and exits are uncannily timed because you read the "mood" of the market better than most.
- **The Disciplinarian:** Your iron will makes volatile markets irrelevant. You stick to your plan, risk is sacred, and emotion never holds sway. This doesn't mean every trade wins, it means wins and losses follow a calculated system, not random whims.
- **The Specialist:** You know one asset type inside and out. Its price drivers, industry influences, and its historical quirks give you a deeper understanding than mere news watchers have, leading to decisive profitable moves.

Unlocking Your Hidden Edge

Many traders don't know where their strongest weapon lies. Here's where your quest begins:

- **Know Your Fear Level:** How much gut-churning volatility can you handle? This dictates appropriate strategies. High risk means high potential reward, but also potential sleepless nights. Be honest, or you'll make trades driven by desperation, not your 'edge.'
- ***Wired For Speed or Strategy?*** Adrenaline junkie or slow-burn analyst? Each needs different tools and setups. Don't force

yourself into a style that goes against your inherent strengths.

- **How Long You Hold:** Day trading requires split-second reactions, while investing builds profits slowly. Your edge MUST align with your holding style, or it's wasted effort.
- **Your Favorite Battlefield:** Some thrive in choppy, fast markets, others excel spotting gradual long-term trends. Don't try to be good at everything - master your chosen terrain.

Sharpening Your Tools: Become One With Your Edge

Once you see those glimmers of your unique strength, sharpen them mercilessly:

- **Get Schooled Where it Matters:** Focus on techniques that AMPLIFY your edge. Technical chart mastery for 'pattern seers,' risk analysis for the cautious, etc. Don't waste time on generic methods.
- **Test It Before Betting Big:** Your edge needs proof in live markets. Start small, track every result, and ruthlessly analyze - is it as consistent as you thought? Or is ego blinding you to flaws?
- **Let Discipline Forge Your Foundation:** Even the best edge dies when emotion seizes control. Strict plan, no deviation - this stops 'gut feelings' from blowing your account.

- **Adapt or Die:** Markets shift, as must your edge. Continual analysis reveals potential areas for improvement - what worked before might not in a new cycle, so learn, adapt, repeat.

Think Like a Trader With a Battle-Tested Edge

Once you know your weapon, your mindset shifts. Success isn't accidental:

- **Knowledge Never Ends:** Strategies age, tools improve, new dynamics arise. Your dedication to constant learning allows your edge to evolve alongside the market, maximizing performance.
- **Humility Avoids Arrogance:** Every edge has limits. Adaptability keeps you winning even when your go-to strategies have a lull. Complacency breeds disaster, flexibility ensures longevity.
- **Risks Become Calculated:** Your edge gives you the confidence to take decisive action when odds are in your favor. Wins aren't guaranteed, but you know WHEN to pull the trigger with high chance of success.
- **Play the Long Game:** Don't sweat short-term setbacks. Edges win over time, through a thousand smart trades, not one lucky gamble. The edge allows you to stay strong during drawdowns, knowing consistency reigns supreme.

Final Challenge

The quest for your edge is never-ending. It's self-examination, strategy work, and relentless adaptability. But like Bruce Lee honing his craft, the effort transforms you from a market 'victim' to a true competitor. And just as the most focused warrior dominates on the battlefield, the focused trader thrives amidst the turbulent tides of finance. Sharpen your weapon, and get ready for victory.

Master Your Instruments

Your Trading Superpower: Knowing Your Tools Inside and Out

Meet Sarah. Smart, follows the rules, has emotional control... yet even when trades technically succeed, profits leave her wanting more. Sound familiar? The issue wasn't in her plan, but that like many traders, she didn't really "get" options. Her mentor Manoj dropped some truth: VIX, those mischievous Greeks - these weren't just fancy terms, but invisible forces pushing her results off-course! Learning their dance transformed Sarah into a profit powerhouse. Here's why that matters:

<u>You Can't Outsmart What You Don't Understand</u>

Imagine trying to win at poker without *quite* grasping the hand rankings. Sure, you might luck out sometimes, but long-term? Same is true with trading. Each instrument - stocks, futures, cryptos, heck, even those complicated option combos - acts like a living thing, with distinct 'personalities' that markets will exploit.

- The Invisible Playmakers: Things like VIX aren't just ticker symbols, they represent trader fear or greed with market-wide influence. That shifts everything about how certain trades behave, without you having a clue why.

- Each Market Has Its Secrets: Forex responds to interest rates, making news reading vital. But stocks care less about that than company earnings reports. Not seeing this keeps you at the mercy of random events vs. informed choices.
- Instrument = Your Battlefield: Some markets are tight, efficient, and your textbook setups work best. Others act chaotic, needing wide stops to catch those wild swings. Using the wrong strategy in the wrong arena is like bringing a knife to a gunfight.

How Deep Knowledge Wins

It's not about memorizing every esoteric fact, but grasping the big picture:

- Anticipation, Not Reaction: When news breaks, you won't be left baffled by price action. You'll see those invisible currents that move your market long before others notice.
- Beyond the Textbook Setup: Every instrument has unique 'tells' for spotting profitable opportunities the untrained eye misses. This lets you pounce on the high-odds trades and filter out the ones likely to just chop you up.
- Managing the Mayhem: A trader who's scared of their own position sizes (because they don't fully grasp the potential price swings) can

never ride out the good trades long enough to see max profit.

How to Achieve Mastery

This stuff doesn't always come by osmosis. Here's what helps:

- Targeted Learning: Find resources focused on your instrument of choice, not generic "get rich" garbage. Those deep dives are more beneficial than skimming it all.
- Follow Those Who "Get It": Find analysts who don't just bark trade calls, but explain the logic *and* how that ties back to the 'personality' of their market.
- Chart Detective Work: Watch historical data even at the expense of a few live trades. How does your instrument respond to news, volume spikes, etc.? You can't cheat that kind of internalized knowledge.

The Bottom Line

Trading can feel like a game rigged against you if you don't understand the playing field. The more deeply you grasp how your chosen instrument ticks, reacts, and acts under pressure, the more you replace pure luck with genuine advantage. It's time well spent in those beginning stages, ensuring that even as concepts get more complex, the foundation holding it all together is rock-solid.

Have a Comprehensive Trading Plan

Picture this: a heart-pounding race, everything's on the line. Skilled drivers battle neck-and-neck, engines roaring. The crowd's going wild, there's pressure from every angle. Sure, a fast car gives you an edge, but who usually stays ahead? It's the driver who can tune out the chaos, keep their cool, and stick to their meticulously crafted race plan. They know every inch of the track, have rehearsed for weather changes, and those pitstop changes are lightning fast. Those drivers don't let adrenaline make them reckless - they rely on preparation to handle those critical moments.

Trading is a lot like that, a mental game as much as anything else. You can't succeed on impulse alone. You need a rock-solid plan to outsmart both the wild market and your own worst enemy - your emotions.

So, What the Heck's a Trading Plan?

It's more than a strategy on paper; it's a battle plan designed to stop you from sabotaging yourself. It's a set of rules and guidelines to keep you anchored when the market storms get rough. A well-made plan eliminates those knee-jerk reactions driven by fear and greed. Think of it as your shield against making costly mistakes out of desperation or hype. It turns you from someone lost in the crowd into a disciplined trader with a clear direction.

Building Your Fortress (Your Trading Plan)

Let's get specific about those defenses. Of course, every trader's plan is unique, but here are some essential components:

- **Your Finish Line (Goals):** Forget vague hopes - get laser-focused. "To grow my account by 5% each month" or "I'm building a downpayment for a house within three years." Short-term goals keep you engaged, long-term goals remind you why you're doing this in the first place.
- **Know Your Limits (Risk Tolerance):** Be brutally honest here. If your trade goes south, where's your breaking point? This dictates not only how big your trades should be but where those ironclad stop-losses go to stop the bleeding fast.
- **Your Trading Style (Methodology):** Are you a chart geek or a news junkie? What market makes your pulse quicken (stocks, forex, options, etc.)? Is your sweet spot short-term swings or long-term holds? All of this molds your specific strategies.
- **Decision Time (Trade Management):** Don't make big decisions during the storm! Your plan pre-decides those for you. Say a stock rockets up 30%, do you hold for more or cash out a chunk? Your plan tells you - based on logic, not emotion.

- **The Journal (Record Keeping & Review):** Track every trade, good and bad. Software, spreadsheet, notebook - the format doesn't matter. It's the analysis that counts. See those patterns, learn what's working, and what's costing you money.
- **Mind Games (The Psychology Bit):** Trading WILL test your patience, mess with your head. Your plan should address this. Maybe you know certain news makes you panic-sell - so your plan might be "avoid all news before market open". Your plan evolves to tackle your weak points.

Why Bother Writing This Down?

- **Fight Your Inner Demons:** Fear, greed, FOMO - every trader knows these beasts. When the urge to panic-sell or blindly chase hype hits, you open your plan, and bam, it hits you: what you *should* be doing, not the impulsive choice.
- **Laser Focus:** A plan isn't just about surviving bad days, it's about thriving. It stops you from chasing every trending stock and jumping between strategies, which is a surefire way to lose. Your plan locks you into what *you* do best.
- **Proof is in the Pudding:** Analyzing trades is how you truly improve. Do your strategies hold up? Seeing it in black and white forces you to adjust, rather than trading on wishful thinking.

Let's Get Started

The hardest step is starting. Find templates, read success stories, but create something that speaks your language. Even a basic plan is miles better than nothing. Think of it like your first clumsy gym workout. You'll get stronger, but the first step is showing up.

Understand the Market Cycles

"Your Perfect Strategy Isn't Always Perfect (Shocking But True)"

Your trusty chart setup hits...and nothing happens. Or worse, the stock tanks! This isn't because the market hates you... it's more likely the market switched moods while you weren't watching. Think of these moods as cycles, and just like your favorite trendy pants, what's hot one year becomes embarrassing the next.

4 Kinds of Market Moods (Yes, Markets Have Feelings Too)

Markets don't actually cry or smile, but they DO show distinct stages that dictate whether your usual setups will shine or flop:

- **Gotta Get It While It's Hot:** Accumulation = smart investors quietly getting back in at the bottom after prices hit rock bottom.
- **Riiide That Wave:** Markup is when trends make money easy to see. Everything works when things are going up consistently.
- **Party's Over (But People Stay Anyway):** Distribution phases are tricky. Volatility is high, but no clear direction...those who got there early sell, while newbies panic-buy the tops.

- **Everyone Leaves in a Hurry:** Markdown (aka bear market) = fear rules. Panic selling outweighs logic, good stocks plummet alongside bad ones.

Why This Messes Up Your Perfect Plan

Here's why cycle awareness is trader superpower:

- **One Trick Ponies Go Broke:** Love momentum trades? Good luck with those in a choppy sideways market. Each phase favors DIFFERENT styles.
- **Even Good Setups Fail Sometimes:** Ignoring the bigger picture leads to frustration. Systems aren't broken, they're just not built for the current "weather".
- **Spotting Opportunity Where Others Lose:** Those who understand "accumulation zone" buying find bargains, while trend-chasers keep selling to them at huge discounts!

Okay, but HOW Can You Figure Out the Market's Mood?

Not magic, more homework:

- **Indexes Don't Lie:** S&P500 tells you overall trend (up, down, messy). Volume spikes also signal big players jumping in or desperately getting out.

- **Sectors Tell Secrets:** Some sectors do well even in bad markets, others lead the charge on rebounds. Who's winning, who's lagging...that's a clue.
- **Economy Does Matter:** Bad jobs reports? Rising interest rates? That colors the market mood, even if an individual stock's fundamentals seem sound.
- **Charts on Bigger Timeframes:** Forget those 5-minute candles for a sec. Those head-and-shoulders tops or broadening bottoms on weekly charts show reversals you'll never spot on minute-by-minute moves.

Being Adaptable Isn't Treason, It's Smart

This means:

- **Bull Time = Trend is Your Friend:** Breakout trades, buying dips with confidence...works as long as the upswing hasn't exhausted itself.
- **Bear Time = Protect That Money:** Shorter trades, iron-clad risk management...scalping may work, but "diamond hands" investing gets slaughtered.
- **Sideways is All About Precision:** Good entries/exits are the ONLY way to profit, or just sit it out (boring, but beats losses)

**Don't Just Trade Stocks, Trade Market *Stages* **

Markets change, strategies should change too. It's NOT about predicting the future, but noticing what's already happening so you're equipped with the right tools for the current fight. This separates those who last a few lucky swings from those who consistently build an account over time.

Stay in Lane

A huge highway,Some cars zip past in the fast lane, others rumble along slowly. Every car gets where it's going, but they each do it differently. Trading's the same way - there's a "lane" out there that's just right for you.

What's Your Trading Lane?

Not sure which lane fits you best? Let's break some options down:

- **Day Trading: Life in the Fast Lane:** Picture lightning-fast decisions, staring at charts all day, jumping on news the second it drops. If you have nerves of steel and love action, this could be your lane.
- **Swing Trading: Catch the Rhythm:** Here, you hold trades for days or weeks, not minutes. It's about spotting trends on the charts, but maybe you take those days to analyze after work, not during the market chaos.
- **Long-Term Investor: Enjoy the Drive:** Company news, financial reports... that's what gets you excited. You don't mind the bumps in the road if you believe in the company long-term. Think years, not days. Patient? This lane might be your jam.

Your Lane Is About More Than Speed

Finding your lane isn't just about fast or slow trades. It's about matching your trading to who you *are*:

- **Risk Rockstar or Cautious Cruiser?** Can you handle those wild swings in the fast lane, or would that turn every trade into a stress nightmare? Be real with yourself!
- **Free Time vs. No Time:** Got hours during the day to watch charts? Perfect. More of an "after work" trader? Your lane will change based on that reality.
- **Personality Matters:** If numbers or charts make your eyes glaze over, forcing yourself into day trading is a recipe for burnout. Love reading company news? Maybe that long-term investing lane makes way more sense.
- **Your Ideal Finish Line:** Are you saving for a downpayment? Looking to turn this into a full-time gig? Different goals mean different lanes.

Hopping Lanes is Hazardous

It's SO tempting to see someone making bank on some strategy and go "Hey, I should do that!" But listen - if it doesn't click with you, it's gonna get ugly fast. Better to figure out *one* lane and get amazing at it.

How to Find Your Sweet Spot:

- **Trading 101:** Books, websites, whatever lets you soak up how each type of trading works. This lets you try things on "in your head" before risking real money.

- **Fake It Till You... Well, Don't**: Practice trades without real money! There are tons of simulators. See which feels most natural for *you*, not what the hotshots do.
- **Feeling Tracker**: When you paper trade (or do the real thing), be honest: were you excited? A nervous wreck? That tells you TONS about the right lane.

The Lane Can Change (Over Time!)

Don't feel stuck in one lane forever. Start learning one method, but know you can adapt it or pick up new ones with experience. Just like in driving, getting confident in the basics makes future learning way easier.

The End Goal: Finding Your Happy Highway

The "best" lane isn't out there, it's the one that works for YOU, your financial goals, and even your mental health. It's where you can be consistent, keep losses small, and spot winners like it's second nature. Don't get distracted by what others are doing, focus on finding that happy highway, and the long-term wins will follow.

Market Structure

"The trend is your friend." - Old Market Adage

Imagine a raging river. Trying to swim against the current is not only a struggle, it's often futile. The same is true in trading. Fighting the momentum of the market is an uphill battle likely to leave you battered and bruised financially. The old market saying, "The trend is your friend," isn't catchy marketing—it's a survival rule.

Trends: The Riverbed the Market Follows

Trends are the underlying pattern in a market's movement. They shape the overall direction, making price action more predictable. Understanding trends requires looking beyond the chaos of individual price changes:

- **Uptrend Anatomy:** A series of higher highs and higher lows reveals a bullish trend. Think of this as water continually eroding a path - making it deeper and easier to follow.
- **Downtrend Dynamics:** Lower highs and lower lows define a downtrend. Like our river example, imagine the force of the current wearing away at a weaker landform.
- **Charting Your Course:** These swings form the visual outline of a trend, like landmarks on a

map. They aren't flawless, but they guide your sense of the market's overall direction.

Why Understanding Trends Holds the Key to Success

Decoding the "trend language" of the market delivers tangible benefits for traders:

- **Trade With the Flow, Not Against It:** Identifying the trend lets you open positions on the market's "preferred" side. It's like getting swept downstream - much easier than fighting your way up.
- **Smarter Risk Management:** Trends give logical places for stop-losses and profit targets. Say the riverbed narrows; that's your signal to limit potential downsides.
- **Trading Without Blind Panic:** Spotting trends lets you focus on higher probability setups, rather than reacting to every little price move. Calm is a great asset in trading.

How to "Learn Fluent Trend"

There's no secret Rosetta Stone for unlocking this skill. Here's where to focus your efforts:

- **Start Simple:** Spend time looking at clean charts— forget indicators for now. Get accustomed to tracking highs and lows and seeing how trends come together.

- **Map the Terrain:** Drawing support and resistance levels visually reinforces the direction and strength of a trend. Think of these as the banks of your metaphorical river.
- **Zoom Out for Perspective:** Remember that a short-term chart may disguise the big picture. Always analyze a trend on multiple timeframes for a broader view of market force.
- **Keep a Trading Diary:** When you think you've spotted a trend, record it. Then track the trade (even if it's just on paper). Did the trend play out as expected?

The Key To Remember

Trend identification isn't an exact science. Sometimes the river splits, sometimes it bends unexpectedly. However, even this basic grasp of direction makes your trades far more intelligent. Learning to read trends gives you a chart-backed opinion instead of being just another trader reacting blindly to random news and noise. In a chaotic market, trends are your best compass for navigating to those sought-after profits.

The Dance of Correlations

"One Bad Supplier Ruins Your Party, Even If YOUR Stock Rocks"

Charts look great, your research sings this company's praises...then it tanks on news about their chip supplier facing delays. It's unfair, but a hard truth of the market: no stock is an island. Here's the problem, and how smart traders use that to their advantage.

Invisible Webs and How They Tank Good Trades

Think of stocks as linked more than you realize, especially when BAD stuff happens:

- **Sectors Fall Together:** An energy price spike? Don't assume only oil companies get rocked, anyone RELYING on those supplies suffers too, in ways less obvious charts alone won't reveal.
- **Domino Effect:** That chip bottleneck doesn't just hurt tech. Companies across industries using those now-rare chips see delays, lost sales...dominoes tumble way further than you'd guess.
- **Fear is Contagious:** Bad economic news creates ripple effects beyond just the stock in focus. Smart money may sell off perfectly good assets to cover losses elsewhere. Logic gets beat by panic.
- **Correlation = Opportunity (Kinda):** Gold goes up when the market tanks, certain stocks tend to

mirror each other...those with sharp eyes catch trends from seemingly unconnected sources.

Who's Really Pulling the Strings

Forget conspiracy theories, this is more about knowing your market players:

- **The Economy is Moody:** Interest rate changes, recession fears...these don't care about your personal research. It influences who invests and WHERE, meaning some sectors get abandoned even if they're solid.
- **It's a Sector Thing:** News hits industries as a whole, even if NOT every company is hurting. Chip stock problems mean less optimism for all things tech, regardless of individual strength.
- **Companies Talk to Each Other...Sort Of:** Big partnerships, reliance on similar supply chains, sometimes just shared infrastructure means your amazing stock gets penalized for their neighbor's mistakes.
- **Social Media IS a Force Now:** Bad press, FOMO around a buzzword...this creates irrational jumps that are just as "real" as actual news in terms of making prices move.

Okay, How Does This Keep Me From Losing My Shirt?

- **Know Your Exposure:** If your amazing play requires certain supplies, or sells mostly to one sector...understand if bad news there ripples to YOU, no matter how good it LOOKS on paper.

- **Correlation = Potential Trades:** Does stock X always jump when Y tanks? That's not magic, it's a pattern to exploit.
- **Diversification Isn't Boring, It's Survival:** Bunch of plays in related industries? One shock may cause them all to suffer simultaneously. Balance your portfolio to spread that risk across areas not likely to ALL react badly at once.

Trade Aware, Not Naive

It's tempting to laser focus on one ticker, pretend everyone else is oblivious pawns. Problem is, they're players just like you, and markets react. Good traders notice the larger choreography - not just who looks pretty onstage, but how the lighting, orchestra, even the crowd can change the entire performance in ways charts don't predict.

You Don't Have to Trade Every Day

The markets are a whirlwind of activity, with a constant barrage of news, opinions, and price fluctuations. It's easy to fall into the trap of thinking you need to be "always on," frantically searching for the next opportunity. But the truth is, successful trading often hinges on knowing when to simply step away.

Why It's Okay (and Often Advantageous) to Take a Break

- **Waiting for Clarity:** Markets go through phases of choppiness and confusion. Trends might break down, technical patterns become unreliable, and volatility becomes excessive. Forcing trades during these murky times leads to sloppy execution and often, losses.
- **Protecting Your Mindset:** Trading is as much a mental game as a technical one. If you're feeling frustrated, burnt out, or overly emotional due to a string of losing trades, it's a prime time to step back. Recharging allows you to come back with a clearer perspective.
- **Enhancing Your Focus:** Successful traders don't rely on gut feelings. They depend on well-defined setups and patterns that offer an edge. If those patterns aren't readily available, your time is

better spent reviewing your strategy or engaging in educational activities.

- **Avoiding Overtrading:** Overtrading is a significant risk, fueled by boredom or the thrill of the action. It can lead to impulsive trades, ignoring your risk management, and ultimately, draining your account.
- **Staying Flexible:** Market conditions change. A strategy that worked well in a hot bull market might struggle during a sideways period. Recognizing and adapting to these changes requires a willingness to step back and reassess.

Overcoming FOMO

Yes, fear of missing out (FOMO) is a powerful emotion. There will be days when a trade you didn't take rockets upwards. But ask yourself this: if that trade didn't fit your predefined criteria, what makes you think the outcome would have been any different for you? Discipline trumps chasing phantom profits every time.

Putting Patience into Practice

Here's how to make patience a key part of your trading toolkit:

- **Define Your Ideal Setups:** Spend time truly understanding what specific patterns, indicators, or market conditions signal high-probability opportunities for your style. If you don't see them, don't force the issue.

- **Schedule "Non-Trading" Time:** Block out specific hours or even days where you won't look at charts. This creates a necessary mental break and prevents impulsive decisions.
- **Focus on Learning:** Use your down-time to sharpen your skills. Study chart patterns, review different trading methodologies, or read up on trading psychology. This strengthens your knowledge base for when high-quality opportunities do arise.
- **Develop Other Interests:** A hobby or interest outside of trading fosters healthy habits and keeps your mind refreshed.

The Big Picture

In the race to become a consistently profitable trader, sometimes the smartest move is not to move at all. Prioritizing patience over action protects your capital, hones your mental focus, and positions you to capitalize when the right opportunities finally emerge. The market will always be there tomorrow; your task as a trader is to preserve your edge for when the time is right to strike.

The Perfect Strategy

"Plans are useless, but planning is indispensable." - Dwight D. Eisenhower

The world of trading can be really exciting, and it's easy to get caught up in the search for the perfect trading strategy. You might imagine that there's a secret formula out there that will help you win every single trade. Unfortunately, this magical strategy doesn't exist. The truth is that all trading strategies have some imperfections, and focusing on finding the perfect one can set you up for disappointment. This chapter will explain why this search is unrealistic and explore the mindset you need to become a successful trader even with those imperfections.

Trading's Inherent Uncertainties

Here's why no trading strategy, no matter how clever, can predict the future perfectly:

- **Dynamic Markets:** Financial markets are always changing. News events, shifting investor attitudes, and economic reports can suddenly change the rules, making a once-reliable strategy useless.
- **Unpredictable People:** While charts reveal patterns, the markets are driven by people, and mass psychology can change unpredictably.

- **Your Own Imperfections:** We're all human! Even with a great plan, emotions like fear and greed can make us hesitate or act impulsively, messing up even the best-designed strategy.
- **The Limits of Backtesting:** Studying past data is important, but even strategies that were profitable in the past might fail in a changed market.

The "Perfect" System Trap

Chasing the dream of the flawless trading system isn't just a waste of time; it can be harmful by making you think this way:

- **The Analysis Paralysis:** You spend so much time on every small detail of your strategy that you never actually take a trade!
- **Fragile Confidence:** Because losses happen to everybody, believing in a "perfect" system makes you think your strategy is broken after just a few losing trades. This leads to panic, not improvement.
- **Missed Opportunities:** Obsessing over a flawless entry point prevents you from noticing real, if slightly imperfect, good trade opportunities.

A Mindset Focused on Process, Not Perfection

Successful traders shift their perspective away from a "perfect" system and focus on these elements:

- **Adaptability is Key:** The market always throws curveballs. Your real skill is your ability to adjust to changing conditions, knowing when to modify your strategy and when to walk away.
- **Focus on the Process:** Invest your energy into defining good entry and exit points, managing risk responsibly, and sticking to your trading plan, not on worrying about individual wins or losses.
- **Expect Drawdowns:** Every trader faces losing streaks. It's just part of the game. Plan for these periods mentally and adjust your trading size to withstand them.
- **Learning Mindset:** Trading is a marathon, not a sprint. Each trade, whether good or bad, teaches you something valuable. Look for lessons and keep making your process better.

Key Takeaway

Chasing the illusion of a perfect trading strategy leads to frustration. Rather than seeking a solution that eliminates losses, accept the uncertainties of the market, adopt a flexible mindset, and commit to honing your trading process day in and day out. Success emerges not from finding an impossible, flawless method, but from being the best at managing those inevitable imperfections, adapting to change, and consistently focusing on your strategic process.

Is It a 'Good' Trade or a 'Bad' Trade?

Beyond Profit and Loss: Is This a 'Good' Trade or a 'Bad' Trade?

Trading can feel like a rollercoaster of adrenaline and doubt. Every flicker on the screen is a decision point: Do you jump in or stay on the sidelines? That split-second urgency can leave traders feeling swept up in the chaos, rather than operating from a calculated mindset. But here's the thing - not all trades are created equal. So, before you hit 'buy' or 'sell,' ask yourself this powerful question: Is this a fundamentally 'good' trade, or a 'bad' one?

What Makes a Trade 'Good' vs. 'Bad'?

Let's go beyond simple labels. Here's how you can dissect the underlying quality of any potential trade:

- **'Good' Trade - Your Strategy's Best Friend:** The heart of this trade aligns with your plan. You've done your homework, noticed specific setups, and understand the risk you're taking.
- **'Bad' Trade - When Emotions Hold the Reins:** Maybe you're desperate to recoup a loss, or FOMO (fear of missing out) has you seeing profits where there's only hype. If emotion is driving the trade, not logic, it's likely a 'bad' one.

- **'Good' Trade - Calculated Risk:** Your plan sets limits, and this opportunity has a good chance of payoff compared to what you're willing to lose.
- **'Bad' Trade - It's a Gamble, Not a Trade:** Forget your stop-loss, risk management takes a backseat because, hey, this just *feels* like it's gonna turn around! Nope. That's the 'bad' trade mindset talking.

Real-World Gut Check: The Apple Dip

Let's get practical. Say everyone's favorite tech giant, Apple, has a weird price drop with no obvious bad news behind it. Buy opportunity, right? Well, it depends...

- **Bad Trade:** Panic-buying without waiting to see if this is a real dip or just random noise. It's tempting, but a lack of analysis is a hallmark of a 'bad' trade
- **Good Trade:** If you specialize in short-term dips, have rules for buying them, and immediately place a stop-loss just in case things keep falling, this might be a 'good' trade decision.

Why Trade Quality Matters More Than Instant Payoff

Understand this: even 'good' trades sometimes result in losses. You can't control the market 100%. And honestly, some impulsive 'bad' trades might net you a quick buck. But what separates lucky gamblers from consistently successful traders is the focus on good decision-making *over time*. Here's why this matters:

- **It's About the Process:** Win or lose on an individual trade, you're building muscle when you stick to good choices. It's a foundation for confidence.
- **Discipline Keeps You in the Game:** Those revenge trades, chasing gains out of boredom, etc. - break all your 'good' trade criteria.
- **Good Losses Teach You:** A 'good' trade that went sideways? That's valuable data, not a crushing blow. Bad trades make you feel hopeless.
- **When Bad Goes Really Bad:** 'Good' trades can turn sour if the market tanks. Recognizing this lets you cut losses instead of turning it into a catastrophic 'bad' trade.

Your Pre-Trade Checklist

Ask yourself these questions before every trade:

- **Gut Check:** Are emotions swaying me, or am I executing a planned strategy?
- **Match Your Plan:** Does this setup honestly fit my established criteria?
- **Risk or Reward?** Be honest: are you only seeing big payouts and ignoring real risk?

- **Contingency**: Where's my stop-loss, and can I stomach that loss if things go wrong?

It's Not About Perfection, It's about the Tilt

Winning every single trade is impossible. But the trader who keeps a disciplined tilt towards 'good' trade choices is the one who keeps improving. They build confidence not from getting lucky, but from knowing why they take each trade - win or lose. Think of this reflection as your internal compass, guiding you toward sustainable success.

Yes ,there is Risk

You find a hot stock. Charts are exploding, it seems every trader online is screaming about it. Dollar signs replace caution...but before you hit "buy", a boring question ruins the fun: "What if this all goes horribly WRONG?"

Traders with Money Left are Obsessed with Losing (Hear Me Out)

Getting into trading seems about making profits - and it is! But veteran traders think deeply about risk long before dreaming about their next vacation. Here's why:

- **Survival IS Victory:** A few disastrous losses can wipe you out. Prioritizing risk control gives you longevity to learn, strategize, and trade for years, not just weeks.
- **Trading Zen: Less Stress, Better Success:** Having pre-planned exits takes emotion out of the equation. When your plan takes over, panic selling and reckless greed stop sabotaging your account.
- **Winning Without Bragging Rights:** Consistent 1-2% gains won't impress your friends... but beating 90% of traders who gamble and blow up IS how you get ahead.

Your Path to Boring Profit Starts Here (It's Simple, Not Sexy)

Before EVERY trade, ruthlessly answer these questions:

- **Where's the Line in the Sand?** Charts reveal when your great idea falls apart. Set a hard stop-loss to cut you off, NOT "hope" the stock bounces back.
- **What's Your Account's Pain Threshold?** No plan is perfect. Risk 1-2% max per trade (even less as a newbie!) so a loss hurts without crippling you.
- **Can You Survive the Streak?** Losing streaks WILL happen. If a few bad trades in a row have you changing your entire strategy, your positions were too large.

NOW Check Potential Profit (Risk Control Unlocks This Step)

Got your risk under control? Fantastic, now see if the potential gain actually justifies it. If the answer is 'no', walking away feels powerful rather than like admitting defeat.

Beyond Rules: Your Brain Matters as Much as Charts

- **Start Tiny, Scale Up:** New to trading? Putting tiny amounts at risk gets you used to the feel of following a plan. Losing $15 sucks, but teaches a valuable lesson without bankrupting you.

- **Sleep is a Profit Indicator:** If position size keeps you up at night, you've taken on too much risk. Calmness leads to wiser choices overall.
- **Journaling Reveals Reality:** Track "why" you entered but also "how" you felt during a trade, especially those painful losses. This builds self-awareness to refine your risk tolerance over time.

It's a Mindset Swap, Not a Magic Trick

Trading ISN'T like the lottery. Gamblers risk it all in one go, often desperately attempting to recover from previous losses. Successful traders have strict parameters, walk away from iffy setups, and always prepare for the "what ifs".

Even Trading Heroes Learned This The Hard Way

Many now-famous traders blew up their accounts early on by ignoring risk. It happens to EVERYONE, regardless of eventual skill. Having a plan and defined limits protects you from repeating those costly mistakes.

FOMO Will Try to Ruin You

Seeing others post huge wins while you sit tight is part of the game. Your discipline in following a plan matters infinitely more than giving in to hype-driven, impulsive trades.

Trading Takes Guts, But Smart Guts

This shift to thinking about loss first is often counterintuitive. But embracing this approach keeps you in the market long enough to actually achieve the gains you visualize. Winning consistently over time is how the money is truly made.

The Art of Risk-Reward Mastery

"Every risk is manageable if you are bold enough to confront it." - William G. Cottrell

Let's be honest, trading is risky business. There's always the chance of losing money, but don't let that scare you off. The key to staying afloat in these choppy waters is learning how to manage those risks smartly. That's where mastering your risk-reward ratio comes in.

What's the Risk-Reward Ratio?

It's a simple idea, but surprisingly powerful. It's all about weighing up how much you could make on a trade (the reward) against how much you might lose (the risk). You figure it out by dividing your potential profit by your potential loss.

Say you've set your sights on a potential $500 profit and your stop-loss (more on that later) limits your downside to $250. That gives you a rock-solid 2:1 risk-reward ratio - for every dollar you risk, you stand to make two back. Now that's something to get excited about!

Why Bother with Risk-Reward?

Here are the top reasons why understanding this principle is so important:

- **Protecting Your Cash:** If you're not careful, a few bad trades can wipe out all your hard work. Focusing on a good risk-reward ratio means knowing when to cut your losses short.
- **Making More Money:** It might sound counterintuitive, but with a focus on higher rewards in your trades, you can be wrong more often than you're right and still make good profits!
- **Staying Sane:** Knowing how much you might lose before you even enter a trade takes a huge weight off your shoulders. That makes for clearer decision-making and less panic-trading.

Putting it all Together

So, how do you use this in the real world? Here's the short version:

1. **Know Your Limit (aka Stop-Loss):** Before you jump into any trade, figure out where you're getting out if it goes south. That's your stop-loss price.
2. **Aim High (Profit Target):** Do your homework and pinpoint a realistic price where you'll pocket your profits.
3. **Do the Math:** Potential profit divided by potential loss. Look for healthy ratios of 2:1 or better!

4. **Stay Disciplined:** It's tempting to jump at any trade that looks halfway decent. But if it doesn't meet your risk-reward criteria, walk away.

Trading in Action: An Example

Imagine two stock trades:

- **1:1 Risk-Reward** Entry Price: $50 Stop-Loss: $45 (Risking $5) Profit Target: $55 (Potential gain of $5)
- **1:3 Risk Reward** Entry Price: $50 Stop-Loss: $45 (Risking $5) Profit Target: $65 (Potential gain of $15)

Now, if you win, let's say, 4 out of 10 trades with that awesome 1:3 ratio, those bigger wins when things go right can easily offset the smaller losses on the other trades.

The Big Takeaway

Mastering risk-reward isn't a magic bullet for overnight riches. But it's a powerful tool to keep you in the game long enough to get better, learn from your mistakes, and find the consistency that separates profitable traders from the rest.

Following Big Money Moves

"Insiders may sell for a variety of reasons, but they buy for only one: they think the price will go up" - Peter Lynch

That sudden stock surge for no reason? Odds are, it wasn't random. Big hedge funds, institutions...their moves shape the market. Problem is, by the time news reports their buys, it's too late for you to catch the wave. Good news: there are ways to track this "smart money" and profit from those shifts.

Whales vs. Minnows: It's Rigged (But You Can Use That)

Let's be honest, they have huge advantages you never will:

- **They Get All the Fancy Rumors:** High-priced research, private calls with companies...average investors learn this stuff long after it impacts the price.
- **Their Trades CREATE Trends:** Their buying (or mass selling) pushes prices in ways no single retail trader ever could.
- **No Panic Button:** When a headline freaks out regular folks, institutions can afford to sit tight. This long-term thinking often means better timing that beats hype-based moves.

How to Find Their Invisible Footprints

It's not about beating them, it's about noticing what they're ALREADY DOING:

- **Volume Doesn't Lie:** Spikes on unusual days, especially combined with bullish candlestick patterns, mean someone big is buying (or the reverse for dumps).
- **Option Peeping Tom:** Unusual activity is tricky, but even basic tools show hints. This takes study, but alerts you to big plays being prepared.
- **SEC Filings are Your Backwards Time Machine:** 13Fs are delayed, but powerful. Seeing a giant pile into a stock you were iffy about is solid confirmation.

Turning This into Actual, Usable Strategy

This doesn't replace good technical analysis, it ENHANCES it:

- **Your Own TA + Smart Money = 🚀:** If your indicators say buy, and volume agrees, your conviction doubles. This prevents hasty fear-sells that lose you gains.
- **Underdogs They Spotlight:** Institutions often find potential BEFORE it hits meme-stock status. Keep an eye on what they're accumulating for early opportunities.

- **Patience Is How You Stay Solvent:** Their holding periods prove why news cycles shouldn't ruin a good setup. It's a boring lesson, but saves accounts.

Don't Forget This Key Fact...

There's a downside to playing at their level:

- **We Get News AFTER They Act:** It's still confirmation of a direction, not a magic buy signal. Price/chart context matters way more than what some billionaire did weeks ago.
- **Tricks Happen:** Big players sometimes try to mislead. Always question motives, don't blindly follow just because it's big money.
- **You're FASTER Than Them:** If you spot a micro-trend forming, a potential breakout that's small for now... institutions miss those. That's YOUR power.

Trade Aware, Not Scared

It's easy to feel like the market is just sharks eating minnows. But even minnows can be clever! Watch their moves not to copy directly, but to spot the currents they CREATE. Then either get carried along the profitable side, or find the little pockets of tasty algae those giants overlook to eat for themselves. This awareness makes the game infinitely more winnable.

Cash is a Position

Markets are tanking, the news is filled with doom...and everyone's rushing to sell. But you? You're oddly calm. See, a chunk of your money is in cash, ready to be used. Time to go shopping while others panic.

Busting the Myth That Cash is "Dead Weight"

A lot of traders think being 100% invested at all times is the goal. But having a good pile of cash on hand isn't lazy, it's the mark of a pro, because it means:

- **Survive the Storms:** When everyone else is forced to sell at deep losses to cover other bills, YOU have the money to wait, or even...wait for it...BUY those amazing discounts.
- **"Sniper Mode" Trading:** Overpriced garbage won't tempt you while cash is burning a hole in your pocket. Suddenly you're the patient hunter, buying only when it's genuinely good, not when panicked people drive things too high.
- **Stress = Bad Trades:** A fat cash balance means you won't freak out in every dip. Calm minds make smart decisions, forced sells often mean mistakes.

Okay, But "How Much" Cash Is Right?

This is where it gets personal, not one-size-fits-all:

- **Your Stomach for Risk:** Hate seeing red in your account? Cash acts as a cushion so you don't panic in every little pullback.
- **What the Market is Doing:** Crazy times might mean being 50% in cash is wise. Smooth uptrend? Less need for a giant "war chest".
- **Are You an Impatient Sort?** Day trader might want cash on hand quicker than someone sitting on stocks for months or years.

Don't Just Sit There, Do Something (Smart) With That Cash

The point isn't to never use it, the point is to be smarter in HOW it's used:

- **Average Down Like a Pro:** Big dip in that awesome stock you always wanted? Instead of lump sum panic-buying, spread that cash out in chunks across several drops. Less stress about timing.
- **Get Paid to Wait:** Some high-yield savings accounts, even short-term bonds, give a few percent. Not amazing, but beats 0% and keeps that buying power safe.
- **Only Hunt The Crazy Bargains:** Holding cash makes you less desperate. If an asset falls way out of proportion, that's when you pounce, not in every 5% market-wide hiccup.

Forget the Market Hustle, Cash Lets You Play it Cool

Everyone loves sounding exciting, like they're "in the fight!". But smart trading has moments of action and moments of planned waiting. Cash gives you freedom. No selling because bills loom, no impulsive moves, just patiently buying awesome opportunities at huge discounts. It's honestly more badass than those stressed-out "all-in" folks.

Trading Discipline

"It was character that got us out of bed, commitment that moved us into action, and discipline that enabled us to follow through." - Zig Ziglar

Picture this: You've identified a stock with textbook indicators signaling an upward surge. Excitement builds as you take a position, envisioning rapid profits. Then, the unexpected happens - the stock drops sharply. Now, your heart hammers. Do you hold tight, hoping for a reversal? Or do you cut your losses with a disciplined exit before things get worse?

This is the crossroads every intraday trader encounters. Discipline is what separates those who consistently turn profits from those who get repeatedly burned by impulsive whims in the market. It's the difference between following your carefully researched rules and letting emotions like fear or greed run the show.

Discipline isn't a personality trait, but a cultivated skill. It involves building habits, mastering self, and consistently choosing actions aligned with your goals, even when tempted to do otherwise.

Why Discipline Builds Winners

- **Shields Against Emotions:** Even seasoned traders feel fear and greed. A clear strategy provides a "compass" when impulses scream contradictory messages, minimizing self-sabotage.

- **The Power of Consistency:** Small daily wins based on a plan compound over time. Impulsive trades deliver erratic returns, lacking the predictability for steady account growth.
- **Enforces Learning:** When each trade is part of a plan, lessons are clearer. Haphazard choices muddy the waters, making it harder to recognize flawed strategies or areas needing improvement.
- **Mental Endurance:** Disciplined trading instills confidence in your system, even during losses. This fortitude allows you to weather market storms without abandoning what has been proven to work long-term.

Pillars of Disciplined Trading

1. **The Holy Grail: Your Trading Plan:** A plan isn't vague intent, but detailed: setups, entries, exits, risk per trade, etc. It prevents trading when emotion rules rather than researched rationale.
2. **Review Rituals:** Your journal logs not just trade details, but the mindset driving them. Regular, brutally honest review forces accountability and refines your approach based on data, not delusion.

3. **Position Sizing as Sanity:** A disciplined trader respects risk rules. Small amounts traded initially preserve capital, build your skillset, and create the psychological space for clear thinking.
4. **Off-Screen Discipline Matters:** How you live fuels how you trade. Proper sleep, exercise, and stress-reduction create the mental clarity needed for sound decisions under pressure.

The Transformative Mindset

Disciplined trading isn't drudgery, it's freedom from:

- The exhausting roller coaster of impulsive trades fueled by fear, greed, and FOMO.
- Relying on external "gurus" or hot tips, taking ownership of your trading journey.
- Constantly questioning your abilities after every loss, instead of focusing on refining a process.

The Takeaway

The market will tempt you to abandon discipline daily. But each moment you resist, you grow not just as a trader, but as a person capable of delaying gratification, mastering your impulses, and achieving long-term goals. Trading is merely the arena where this personal growth yields substantial benefits.

Why Discipline Defeats Chaos

- **Safeguarding Against Emotion:** We're all human. Panic as prices reverse and irrational exuberance after a quick gain are easy traps to fall into. Discipline gives you a framework of pre-set entry and exit points, limiting the chance of hasty selling at the bottom of a dip or clinging onto a losing trade long past its logical conclusion.
- **Consistency Breeds Profits:** Market chaos makes short-term movements unpredictable. When you consistently follow a proven strategy, results stabilize over time, even amidst temporary turmoil.
- **Learning from Mistakes:** Losses are part of the game. The trick is not letting them lead you down a spiral of doubt or impulsive revenge trades. Discipline forces rational analysis, turning past failures into invaluable lessons for refining your future approach.

Building Your Discipline Muscle

- **The Trading Playbook:** Draft a detailed trading plan with clear rules for when to buy, when to sell, how to size positions, and how to use protective stop-losses non-negotiably. Refer to this script before every trade to prevent emotional improvisation.

- **Trading Journal:** Honesty with yourself is paramount. Diligently documenting your wins, losses, and most importantly, the thought process behind every trade exposes patterns. Are you consistently ignoring stop-losses or chasing unsustainable momentum? Your journal can't lie, paving the way for conscious correction.
- **Small Steps, Big Gains:** Begin with very small trade sizes. This eases psychological pressure, letting you focus purely on executing your planned actions rather than worrying about losing substantial amounts. As your discipline muscle becomes reliable, you can comfortably increase your position sizes gradually.

Your Transformation

Just imagine...instead of a rollercoaster of self-doubt and impulsive decisions in response to every price wobble, you trade with calm rationality. Stop-losses act as shields, minimizing the stress of bad trades. Each decision is anchored in your tried-and-true plan. This unwavering discipline empowers you to stay within your strategy, even when the market temporarily throws a curveball. With this unshakeable approach, you see results gradually shift: less impulsive reactions, a smaller number of lost trades, and steadily growing profits.

Conclusion

In the beginning, trading with discipline might feel restrictive. However, think of it as building a robust foundation for enduring success. Your well-crafted plan gives you freedom from emotionally-fueled chaos. The more you hone your discipline, the more successful you become. And that, more than the most exciting single-day profit, is what intraday trading is all about.

The philosophy is simple but profound: strive to be the most disciplined person in the room, and you're on the path to becoming the best trader in the room.

Simplicity

Let's face it, we've *all* been tempted to go a bit indicator crazy. Those squiggly lines and flashy signals whisper promises of trading superpowers. But piling them on without strategy rarely ends well. Here's the thing: too much "analysis" often just masks problems you may not want to admit. Here's the deeper damage that can be done:

- Dodging The "I Don't Really Get It" Problem: Indicators let you feel like you have a system, even if you're secretly fuzzy on market basics. But without that grasp of price action patterns and support/resistance zones, you're just blindly trusting wiggles instead of developing genuine skill.
- Confusing Activity with Success: It's strangely exciting to watch a dozen indicators go wild during a big market move. But remember, that reactive chaos isn't the same as being able to identify profitable setups or knowing when to exit a trade *before* the indicators give a lagged signal.
- Recipe for Emotional Trading: When things don't align, that anxiety mounts. You may jump in too early just to make the conflicting signals stop, take impulsive exits because you can't handle the mixed messages, or freeze entirely

while watching a good opportunity come and go. All that is the opposite of calm, logic-driven trading.

- Death By a Thousand Tweaks: Overfitting - tweaking every indicator endlessly until it performs perfectly on old data - isn't research, it's self-delusion. You create a hyper-specialized system bound to collapse the moment a market shift throws it a curveball.

The Path to Clearer Charts (and Trading):

While a select few indicators are vital, remember:

- Mastery, Not the Magic Combo: Truly skilled traders often work with very few tools, because they prioritize the market data itself over layered confirmation. It takes work to get confident at those chart basics, indicators can't substitute.
- Indicators Confirm, Not Contradict: See a strong downtrend, but one indicator's optimistic? That's not a 'go' sign, it's a reason to look deeper, find out why that one tool disagrees with the current context.
- Less = More (Confidence Boost Included): As counterintuitive as it sounds, removing all but your core indicators for a week forces you to truly learn what the chart itself is telling you. Once you see it's possible to survive without

the visual reassurance, you'll gain respect for using them sparingly.

- Backtesting Therapy: See where your favorites fail historically. This removes a lot of their mystique! No tool is immune to changing market conditions, and that reality check helps you use them strategically, not with blind faith.

The Bottom Line

If your charts look like a techno-rainbow vomited up all the math equations your brain suppressed in high school, it's time to simplify. It's okay to start by adding one indicator, observing it over time, and gradually growing from there as your knowledge of both the indicator and the underlying market develops.

Patience in Trading

"Patience is bitter, but its fruit is sweet." - Aristotle

Imagine that leopard perched in the tree, blending seamlessly with the dappled sunlight. Every sense is finely tuned, not to every flicker of movement below, but to the specific signs of its chosen prey. Hours might pass, yet it does not pounce at squirrels or dart after fleeting birds. It waits, conserving its energy and focus, poised for the *perfect* opportunity.

Successful intraday traders need that same patient focus. The market is a swirling whirlwind of potential - prices surge, then plummet in the blink of an eye. It's so easy to fall for that frantic urge to be in on *something, anything,* right now. But true trading skill means knowing when to pounce, and when to hold back.

Think about that trader glued to their screen, jittery with frustration. The market seems to explode with movement, while they sit on the sidelines. Those posts bragging about big wins eat away at their discipline... surely there's something to trade! Then, out of fear of missing out, they dive into a setup, just as the momentum falters. Panic selling and losses replace the hope of gains.

Sound familiar? We've all fought that battle to some extent. Patience is the hardest skill to master because the market makes it feel like you're losing when you're sitting still. However, true patience separates consistent winners from those who burn bright and quickly flame out.

Patience: Your Competitive Advantage

- **Wait for YOUR Trade:** Not every flicker of price action is worth risking your money on. Impatience fuels sloppy, unplanned trades, breaking your carefully built strategy. Patience preserves both your mental energy and your trading capital.
- **Let the Winners Roar:** When you strike too early, your profits get capped early too. Patience lets those good trades build into true momentum and bigger payouts.
- **Tough Skin Training:** Trading will dish out losses, it's unavoidable. Patience turns frustration into focus. Losses become lessons, not triggers for emotional revenge trades.
- **Adapt When it Counts:** Markets constantly change. Sometimes they rage, sometimes they drift sideways. Patience helps you tune into those rhythms, only pouncing when conditions are perfectly suited to your strategy.

Develop "Leopard Level" Patience: Strategies for Today

- **Start Small for Big Results:** Patience is a habit. Smaller starting positions ease the pressure, letting you practice resisting the urge to jump in prematurely.

- **Your Journal is Your Reality Check:** Re-reading past losses triggered by impulse is painful, but that pain makes you sharper and less likely to repeat the same mistakes.
- **Life Beyond Charts:** Time not staring at screens builds the mental clarity needed for good trading. Meditation, hobbies, anything that gives you calm keeps you from overreacting in the moment.

Two Traders, Two Journeys:

Picture this:

- **The Patient Trader:** Enters only when their proven setups form flawlessly. Objectively analyzes losses and learns. Over time, they steadily scale up as consistency becomes their superpower.
- **The Impatient Trader:** Constantly jumps into trades fueled by FOMO and anxiety. Losses deepen because they try to "trade back" every setback. Short-lived gains can't offset the deep drawdowns.

The Bottom Line

Everyone talks about wanting quick riches, but that approach rarely lasts. Trading is a long game. And it makes sense - who usually wins a marathon? Yes, there's the occasional burst of speed, but real, sustained success goes to the one with the discipline to pace themselves. Learn to master the art of being patient, striking strategically, and you'll avoid the mistakes that make so many traders flame out.

Keep it Physical

Picture the scene: another tough trade bites the dust. It's tempting to erase the evidence, swipe the loss under the rug, and immediately chase a new setup. But you take a different path. Instead of hitting that "buy" button, you reach for a weathered notebook, a pen poised above the pristine page.

"March 14th, 10:17 AM, Sold XYZ short, 200 shares..." With this deliberate act, you begin journaling - but this isn't just some mindless list of trades. You're building a powerful weapon: a physical record of your decisions that forces self-examination in a way a spreadsheet rarely does.

Why Pen and Paper Pack a Punch

- **It's Not Just Data, It's Connection:** Typing notes feels sterile. Ink on the page makes the trades and their outcomes feel tangible, helping you internalize the consequences and potential causes more deeply.
- **Mindfulness vs. MindLESSness:** Writing by hand demands presence. Each deliberate stroke forces you to analyze elements of the trade you might otherwise gloss over in the frantic rush to "be back in the game."
- **A Sanctuary from Overwhelm:** Trading platforms hum with distractions. Your

notebook is just for reflection. No flashing charts, just you, the trade, and a place to parse through what drove the choice, good or bad.

- **Your Trading Legacy, Unedited:** Over time, this ledger becomes something special. An unfiltered timeline charting not just trade specs, but the evolution of your skillset and the refinement of your approach.

Setting Up Your Masterpiece

- **Tools Are Personal:** It's NOT about fancy stationery. You want a durable notebook, pages that won't smear, and a style that encourages frequent use. Grid layouts might suit those who like organized data entry.
- **Core Facts + Your Commentary = the Gold:** Journal consistently, logging basics: symbol, entry/exit prices, sizes, etc. BUT the secret sauce is in those 'notes': "Stopped out early, felt fear taking over", or "Didn't take news into account". That self-examination is invaluable later.

Leveling Up with Your Journal

- **Consistency = Clarity:** Build this into your routine. Immediately after exiting a trade, while emotions are still fresh, record it. Accuracy improves, making those patterns over time easier to spot.

- **Brutal Truth, Not Self-Delusion:** Journaling your mess-ups isn't so you can beat yourself up later. It's so you can't sugarcoat them away, making fixing the habits causing them faster.
- **Weekly Debriefs:** Read past entries - not just trade stats, but those notes on WHY you acted. That's where you suddenly catch yourself saying, "I keep taking profit too early..." which reveals tweaks needed.

Your Journal Evolves - Just Like You

The beauty is, with dedicated use, it transforms. Day 1 entries feel rudimentary next to those 6 months in where you start noting how market conditions subtly affect your psychology. This growth chart has power no platform can replicate.

Important Notes:

- **It's a Supplement, Not a Replacement:** A dedicated notebook doesn't make your charting tool obsolete. This is the deeper layer beneath the technicals.
- **Analysis Can Be Tedious:** It's more work to manually record vs. apps auto-populating trades. If journaling feels like torture, you won't do it, losing the benefit.

The Bottom Line

In a world dominated by screens, there's magic in the physical act of putting your trading history to paper. You engage with trades differently, making hidden flaws harder to ignore. For some, it's the key to the kind of growth no indicator or analysis platform alone can match. Give it an honest try, that tattered notebook may become worth its weight in saved losses and accelerated skill.

Don't Try to Outsmart the Market

This Is Why Your "Genius" Trading Ideas Usually Blow Up

You found a loophole! A chart pattern nobody noticed, a news cycle about to swing a whole sector your way. It's tempting to think "I'll beat the system, outsmart Wall Street". But before you go all-in on your brilliant idea...take a deep breath. The market usually crushes that kind of arrogance.

The Market Does Not Care About Your Ego

Harsh but true: here's why trying to always be the smartest guy in the room backfires when trading:

- **You Don't Know What You Don't Know:** Big investors see stuff you never will. Algorithms move faster than you can blink. Trying to compete on "intel" means losing before you begin.
- **Everything Is (Mostly) Priced In:** If it's public info, odds are it's already impacted the stock. "Hidden gems" stay hidden for a reason, they usually suck or will get found fast by others and surge out of your reach.
- **"I Saw a Pattern!" No, You Probably Didn't:** Brains love finding order in chaos. Most of the time, it's confirmation bias (seeing what you were

primed to see), or dumb luck disguised as brilliance.

Overthinking Becomes Your Worst Enemy

Even if you're not convinced the market is smarter, YOU often sabotage your own trading, here's how:

- **Paralysis by Analysis:** Good setup, but then one news headline freaks you out, missed move. Happens constantly. Simple plans beat overcomplicating every scenario.
- **"But But the Fundamentals!"** Sometimes a pump happens just because everyone ELSE gets excited. Fighting the crowd instead of going with the flow usually burns you.
- **Everyone Else Seems Excited...** Chasing that stock Twitter shills about means buying high, selling low. FOMO makes traders forget good entries matter more than stock hype.

"So...How DO I Make Money Then?"

Good question! Successful trading has zero to do with magic secrets, more about discipline:

- **Work WITH the Market, Not Against It:** Strong trends exist for a reason. Trying to be a contrarian means missing easy profits for the sake of feeling clever.
- **Cut. Those. Losses:** Being wrong costs money, being STUBBORNLY wrong blows up your account. The market ain't apologizing, adapt or die.

- **Boring Wins Over Flashy:** Clear strategy, good risk management...sounds tedious next to that hot stock tip. But consistent small wins outlast those "once in a lifetime" gambles 99% of the time.

Market Cycles Happen, Get on Board or Get Crushed

There will be bull runs and bear markets. Accept this, don't get mad the rules change. What matters is sticking with your plan regardless of the overall mood because guess what? Conditions ALWAYS shift back eventually. Trying to time those shifts ends badly.

The Market Doesn't Play Fair, That's the Point

If everyone could get rich easily, nobody would work a regular job. Outsmarting the market is a fantasy that makes you take stupid risks instead of focusing on proven methods tailored to your risk tolerance and goals. Embrace that truth, and maybe that brilliance actually has a chance to be used constructively.

Avoid Tomorrow's Headache

"We are what we repeatedly do. Excellence, then, is not an act, but a habit." - Aristotle

Imagine a trader tempted to deviate from their trading plan. Instead of riding a winning position according to their system, they take an early profit out of fear the market will reverse. While it feels good to pocket a short-term gain, that action sets in motion several negative outcomes: the trade doesn't reach its full potential, their confidence in letting winners run weakens, and it steals capital from potentially bigger winners they could now only take smaller positions on.

In the intensity of the moment, it's easy to view each trade in isolation. However, successful traders understand the deep interconnectedness of their actions. Today's impulsive exit, ignored drawdown warning, or overleveraged bet casts a long shadow, both practically and psychologically, on your future opportunities. Recognizing this cultivates a profound sense of responsibility in each trading decision.

The Practical Ripple of Every Trade

Your past trades aren't just statistics, they directly impact your future trading:

- **Capital Preservation vs. Erosion:** Reckless losses don't simply reduce your trading account today, they limit the opportunity to compound on wins. It requires far more future profits to merely break even from foolishly surrendered gains.

- **Sizing Constraints:** Blowing risk management rules creates holes you need to dig out of. To regain lost equity, subsequent trades have to be either riskier or smaller, both suboptimal strategies for building an account.
- **"House Money" Trap:** Even "winning back" a big loss through aggressive risk-taking is dangerous. Playing with winnings you psychologically don't own leads to even looser decision-making.

The Mind of the Long-Game Trader

Understanding the ripple effects molds a trading mindset centered on sustainability:

- **Process Over Single Outcomes:** One wildly successful or damaging trade makes for entertaining stories, but doesn't determine your career. It's consistent adherence to your system over time that yields actual results.
- **Emotional Contagion:** Impulsive trades breed more impulsiveness. Letting greed or frustration get the better once sets a precedent the mind likes to repeat until harsh losses break the cycle.

- **The Opportunity Cost:** Exiting too early for small gains not only limits that trade's profit, it steals capital from potentially even higher-reward setups lurking on your watchlist.

Cultivating a Forward-Looking Approach

Here's how to ensure today's actions propel you forward, not hold you back:

- **Metrics Beyond Money:** Track trade adherence to your plan alongside wins/losses. Rewarding "good behavior" creates positive reinforcement, making process as vital as profits.
- **The Post-Loss Autopsy:** Don't just see red on your dashboard, but analyze precisely where you went wrong. Every losing trade, however painful, reveals an area for improvement.
- **Scenario Planning:** Ask not just "how will I profit on this trade," but "what impact does this potential entry size have on my overall positioning, future opportunities, and even the worst-case outcome I can stomach?"

Trade as if Your Future Self is Watching

Imagine you could teleport the results of your trading activity ahead six months. Seeing that impulsive trades had lasting negative consequences might cause you to re-think your strategy! Each trade you take creates that future.

- **Small Compromises Add Up:** Violating stop-losses by small percentages, giving back profits bit by bit, or not letting winners run add up to far less wealth potential over time.
- **Building Healthy Patterns:** Every time you execute according to plan, it strengthens that behavior. Success requires not just knowledge, but the discipline ingrained by repetitive action.
- **Reputation to Yourself:** Your greatest trading asset is your mental capital. Knowing you make impulsive, destructive decisions erodes confidence, which in turn breeds more bad decisions. Keep your word to yourself.

The Takeaway

Trading is a marathon, not a sprint. It's easy to let a string of losses or big wins warp your approach. Each decision reverberates far beyond the execution of a single trade. Thinking of today's actions as directly impacting your tomorrow empowers a mindset prioritizing consistency, calculated risk, and a laser focus on the long-term success only this deliberate approach can achieve.

Buffer Capital: Your Financial Lifejacket

"Risk comes from not knowing what you're doing." Wise words from Buffett, and it applies directly to trading! That's why having some "breathing room" in your trading account is vital - even if it feels like wasted money at first.

Your 'Oops, That Didn't Work Out' Fund

Okay, imagine this: You feel like a trading genius. The charts look amazing, all the stars are aligned, and you're ready to bet the farm on one amazing trade! But what if things don't pan out?

That's where buffer capital comes in! It's money you set aside within your trading account, but it's strictly hands-off - your emergency stash for when the market throws a curveball. Say you have $10,000 to trade, a good buffer could be $2,000-$3,000. You only make trades with the other $7,000.

Why "Waste" the Extra Cash? Here's Why:

- **Markets Be Crazy:** Even the best get it wrong sometimes! Your buffer means one bad call doesn't wipe you out.
- **Stress is the Enemy:** A losing trade stings, but without a buffer, that panic messes with your head. You risk ditching your good plan in

desperation. A buffer lets you breathe, learn, and keep calm.

- **Confidence Wins:** Knowing one loss won't ruin you makes you less nervous. You trade smarter, not harder.

How Much Buffer Do *I* Need?

This part's personal:

- **Scaredy-Cat or Daredevil?** If you hate risk, your cushion needs to be bigger to keep you sane! More confident traders could go a bit smaller.
- **Short-Term vs. Slow & Steady:** Risky day trades need bigger safety nets than those long-term investments.
- **Trading Newbie:** When you're learning, a healthy buffer makes those early mistakes much less painful.

Don't Go All-In! (At least, not in the beginning)

It's tempting when you see that "perfect" setup, but hold back. Slow and steady wins the race, and your buffer keeps you in the game long enough to figure out what works. Your future self will thank you.

The True Power of Buffer Capital

Buffett understood risk in a deep way. Trading WILL have losses, but by being smart about how much you shield off, you'll learn tons from those losses. That's what helps you actually improve! Your buffer isn't just protecting your cash, it's like training wheels for your trading mindset - they come off when you're riding that sweet winning streak!

"Bottom Fishing" and "Top Sniping":

You see that chart plummeting. A little voice whispers, "This HAS to be the bottom. Time to buy the dip!" Then... nothing. It keeps dropping, leaving you frustrated, the trade a loser. Sound familiar?

Why We Love Extremes (And Why It's Dangerous)

We're humans, we like drama. "Calling the top" or "buying the absolute bottom" sounds heroic. Plus, trading can mess with your head - sometimes we care more about being RIGHT than actually making money.

The Problem with Being a Perfectionist

Here's why trying to time markets down to the penny is a losing game:

- **No One's a Fortune Teller:** Charts might give clues about reversals, but no one is psychic. Exact timing? Pure luck.
- **Missed Moves = Missed Money:** Fixating on the "perfect" price means you often miss big trending moves. Even getting in a bit 'late' beats losing money fighting the trend.
- **Your Brain Hates This:** "What if it drops lower?" "Did I buy too soon?" This fear and self-doubt is how bad decisions get made.

Shift Your Focus: Be a Trend Spotter, Not a Psychic

Winning traders make money off what's actually happening, not what they wish would happen.

- **The Trend is Your Friend:** If it's going up, keep buying more on the way up. Same logic for downtrends - why fight it?
- **Charts Aren't Magic, But They Do Help:** Moving averages, trendlines...tools exist so you're reacting to data, not just gut feelings.
- **Don't Bet the Farm:** Instead of one "perfect" buy, get in pieces as the trend confirms. Less risk, better average price.

Don't Fall for the "Missed Move" Hype

Sure, sometimes a stock skyrockets AFTER you got in. But wouldn't you rather make some profit than none at all chasing an imaginary low point? Nobody goes broke taking profits, but people DO go broke trying to guess where every last reversal happens.

It's Not About Being Perfect, It's About Staying Alive

Perfect timing is a myth. Markets change, there's ALWAYS money to be made somewhere. Stop dreaming of catching the peak, and start actually reacting to trends you can see with your own eyes. That's how you make trading boring, steady...and profitable.

Greed Trap in Trading

How Greed Turns Winning Trades into Losers (And How to Fight Back)

That feeling when a stock is flying way past your profit target...that's greed knocking. "Maybe it'll double from here!" whispers the voice in your head. Then, suddenly it reverses, wiping out gains, sometimes turning a winner into a loser. Been there?

Greed Isn't About Money, It's About Sabotage

Greed ain't just wanting more - it's when good trading habits die. No risk control, ignoring your planned exit strategy...this ain't ambition, it's account suicide. Greed shows up in sneaky ways:

- **"Diamond Hands" Gone Wrong:** You hit your goal, but now it HAS to keep going higher. Forget celebrating, your winner might become a loser before you know it.

- **Betting the Farm:** Suddenly your position size is way bigger, leverage makes you reckless. One bad trade doesn't just sting, it can wipe you out completely.

Greed Loves to Mess With Your Head

Here's why it's easy to fall into the trap:

- **Ego Boost:** Quick wins make you feel invincible. Suddenly your usual cautious plan looks boring.
- **"What If" Madness:** You see those gains piling up, then start focusing on what you MIGHT make with just a bit more risk. Greed gets you mad at good trades for NOT making you a millionaire overnight.
- **FOMO Fueled by Social Media:** Every influencer got rich today, so why can't you? That pressure leads to taking stupid chances with your actual savings.

Your Anti-Greed Toolkit

Winning the greed battle takes conscious effort and some willpower:

- **Boring Planning Saves Exciting Profits:** Before buying, know your exit point for BOTH good and bad trades. Chart levels, NOT emotions, should dictate when you say goodbye.
- **Stop Losses Are Sacred:** These orders are there so your brain doesn't sabotage you. No widening stops to justify holding a loser you secretly know should be closed.
- **Eat the Cake in Chunks:** "Scaling out" lets you lock in some profit along the way. Less pressure to be superhuman and less regret if it plummets.

Trade For Survival, Not Sudden Wealth

The promise of easy riches? That's greed's sales pitch. But it either kills you quick in one bad trade or bleeds you dry slowly. Consistent winners protect their money, they don't gamble it on delusions of grandeur.

Don't Be Ashamed, This Happens to Everyone

Trading isn't just about getting trades right, it's about controlling your mind. Know your profit goals, have an exit plan, and remember: It's better to make consistent 'good' money than have crazy swings between genius and bankrupt.

Be a Good Loser

"Every Bad Trade Is Tuition You Paid... Are You Going to Class?"

Red flashes on the screen. That trade you were SO sure about? Tanking. It's easy to be mad at yourself, at the market... it's even tempting to double down with "revenge trading" to somehow erase the loss. But that's how good traders become gamblers. Loss is part of the process, what separates the winners is how they handle it.

Forget "Winning". You Need to Master Bouncing Back

Trading, like life, has setbacks. The question isn't IF that will happen, it's how it shapes your next move. This ain't just feel-good fluff, it's cold hard trader math:

- **Every Loss is a Clue:** Didn't see that reversal coming? Risked too much on one play? Losing shows where your plan sucks. Don't waste that valuable info!
- **Emotions Ruin Accounts, Not One Bad Trade:** The real danger isn't losing money, it's letting that derail your whole mindset. Fear and tilt lead to dumb trades, breaking free of that wins long-term.

- **Get Realistic, or Stay Broke:** Thinking every trade should win means two things: unrealistic expectations and panic when it doesn't. This makes it impossible to trade effectively.

How a Smart Trader Digests a Loss

Think of a loss as an expensive class you HAD to take, now get the most out of it:

- **Journal Like Your Future Success Depends on It:** Don't just fume, put those feelings into detailed notes. What you saw, what you missed, even how you felt at the time - patterns will emerge.
- **Spot Your Bad Habits:** Did you panic-sell, let ego override your plan? Consistent losses signal where you need to train yourself, not rewrite your whole strategy.
- **Tweak, Refine, Repeat:** One loss doesn't mean everything is garbage. It likely means tighter stop-losses, clearer entry signals, or even adjusting markets you trade to match your mindset.

Resilience Isn't a Gift, It's a Skill You Practice

Losing money (which WILL happen) sucks. But feeling sorry for yourself doesn't fix it. Learning from it means the next trade isn't based on fear, but calculated analysis influenced by experience those blow-out traders will always lack. That's your advantage.

Trading is About Being Bent, Not Broken

Embrace setbacks as tests designed to make you unbreakable. Markets move on, stocks recover, losses become lessons. It's tempting to sit and dwell, to declare all of this "not for you" when it goes sour. But instead of quitting in anger, quit out of boredom when you get so good you handle failures as minor distractions - that's how wealth is built.

Perils of Averaging Down in Trading

"The stock market has a mind of its own, and trying to guess what it will do next is futile." - Gerald M. Loeb

Imagine a trader buying into a stock they believe in. The price falls, tempting them to buy more at the lower price...and falls again. Lured by the promise of an eventual rebound, they "average down," buying more and more shares to reduce their average entry point. It's a familiar strategy, one that can amplify both rewards and dangers.

Averaging down can be profitable but should be approached with the caution one extends towards a deceptively tempting siren call. Under specific circumstances, it's a tool. Misunderstanding its risks, however, can lead to financial ruin.

Why Averaging Down Can Be a Double-Edged Sword

- **Potential for Profit...:** If the stock recovers, your average entry price is lower, meaning you gain back losses faster and reach profitability sooner. This strategy aligns well with long-term, value-based investment philosophies.
- **...Or Prolonged Pain:** If the stock continues to sink, you pile up shares in a losing position. Not only are losses mounting, but you've tied up capital that could be better deployed elsewhere.

- **Missed Opportunities:** While you sink money into a declining stock, you might miss profitable trends elsewhere. Diversification and opportunity cost awareness are critical.
- **Distorted Psychological Perspective:** Averaging down often arises from an unwillingness to admit an initial judgment was wrong. It can make exiting a bad trade (and cutting losses) even more difficult.

When Averaging Down is Most Dangerous

- **Trading Without a Stop-Loss:** Averaging down becomes infinitely more reckless without predefined exit points. Having safeguards protects your capital from being entirely decimated in an unrecoverable decline.
- **Catching Falling Knives:** Averaging down into fundamentally weak companies or those under immense pressure is unwise. It's often less about value and more about attempting to outsmart a downward trend.
- **Emotional Attachment:** If the decision stems from desperation to "not be wrong" rather than reasoned analysis, averaging down is likely a disastrous move born of self-deception.

Averaging Down Thoughtfully (If at All)

- **Deep Conviction:** Only consider a stock in which you have fundamental belief for reasons beyond a recent price drop. Extensive research and due diligence are necessary to ensure you're not pouring money into a sinking ship.

- **Technical Signals:** Look for support levels or potential reversal signs along with your average-down plan. Buying blindly into a downtrend rarely pays off.
- **Limited Deployment:** If you do take this route, allocate only a small portion of your capital. This acknowledges the heightened risk associated with this strategy.

The Takeaway

Averaging down can be a tool, but like any tool, it requires skilled craftsmanship. It's often wiser to admit a mistake, accept the loss, and redeploy capital strategically rather than chase a failing position driven by emotion or stubbornness. In an arena guided by data and risk assessment, letting pride dictate decisions usually ends in painful lessons.

Never Let a Day Trade Turn into a Swing Trade

The "Just Hold It Overnight" Trap

You know exactly how this feels. Planned day trade goes sideways, red starts creeping in... You get that little voice: "It'll bounce back tomorrow... right?" Suddenly, "get in, get out" turns into a whole mess of uncertainty. It seems harmless, but it messes with your entire trading day.

Day Trading Ain't Swing Trading (And That's a Good Thing!)

Here's why that one decision is bad news, even if it feels "minor":

- **Day Trades: In and Out.** Charts, short-term patterns, that's what you prepared for. You pick those battles based on specific rules made for quick action.
- **Swing Trades: Hold That Tiger.** Here, you're okay with multi-day swings. News matters more, the chart looks totally different from your usual day-trade setup. This takes way more patience.

When Your Brain Lies to You

Changing the rules mid-game gets dangerous, fast:

- **Oops, Forgot About Risk:** That stop-loss that made sense at 10 AM? Useless if it plunges down while you sleep. You haven't mentally prepped for a larger potential loss.
- **Analysis? Out the Window:** Did you actually look at this as a swing opportunity? No, you were busy making panicked day-trading decisions on the fly. This is setting yourself up for failure.
- **Missing What You're Actually Good At:** While one trade eats away at you, better setups (for your skills) go by unnoticed. Your funds and focus are tied up in something you now barely understand.

How Not to Do This to Yourself

It takes practice, but here's how you fight this sneaky impulse:

- **Decide Before You Buy:** Is this a "quick profit" trade or a longer play with some news risk or earnings coming up? Be honest with yourself and analyze with *that* goal in mind.
- **Time Really Can be Your Stop-Loss:** If it's not moving up like it should by certain time (your choice!), get out. Doesn't matter if it's green or red, the point is: your plan failed, respect it.

- **Lists Are Your Friends:** Keep 'day trade' and 'swing watchlists' separate. When you feel the urge to cross things over, stop - ask yourself which list this even belongs on to clarify your thinking.

The Real World Ain't Perfect

There ARE times plans gotta change. Maybe the stock goes crazy after hours, something amazing happens suddenly. But if that's the exception, not the rule, get in the habit of closing losers at your normal trading day end.

You, But Smarter

Trading's not about one trade getting it right, it's about sticking to the types of setups you can actually win at. Day trading and swing trading BOTH work, but it gets ugly when you don't decide WHICH you're doing beforehand. Don't set yourself up to panic mid-trade... that's how losses stack up and your confidence gets shot!

Skill vs. Luck in Trading

Today You're a Genius, Tomorrow the Market Thinks You're an Idiot

Victories do create that heady "trading god" feeling. But even if some skill played a role, luck whispers sweet nothings into your ear. Let's break down why keeping luck in your peripheral vision means the difference between sustainable wealth and painful lessons:

Skill vs. Lucky Breaks (How to Not Lose Everything)

A single trade is a cocktail, shaken in different proportions:

- **Skill = Knowledge PUT INTO ACTION:** Your refined technical analysis, market news evaluation, and unwavering adherence to your trading plan - those are skills you diligently develop.
- **Luck = Chaos You Can't Plan For:** Unexpected positive earnings reports benefiting your holdings, an unforeseen market-wide dip right before your stop-loss - both pure luck.
- **Probability IS Your Friend:** A consistent edge (with big wins outweighing small losses) doesn't mean infallibility. Trading's a long game where skill prevails as luck's influence gradually weakens.

Why Your Ego Is a Liability

Denying luck makes you vulnerable:

- **Win Streaks Lie:** Luck inflates a hot streak into a perceived mastery of the markets. Risk tolerance skyrockets, positions balloon, and when luck inevitably evaporates, you're caught overexposed.
- **Bad Days Crush Your Soul:** False certainty in your brilliance makes losses seem like proof of incompetence. Skilled strategies get discarded after brief periods of market unfavorability, destroying hard-won confidence.
- **Misplaced Pride Turns Losses into Catastrophes:** Ego makes you hold onto losers (it MUST turn around!) or jump prematurely into revenge trades to 'prove' yourself. Both spell doom.

Real Skill Lets You Survive All Market Moods

While occasional, luck-induced pain or joy happens to everyone, skill-driven traders thrive long-term by:

- **Never Stop Learning:** Analyze each trade, win or lose, with equal scrutiny. Market patterns evolve; staying ahead of the curve protects you from outdated methods.
- **Risk Rules Are Like Traffic Signals:** You respect limits even when sailing on an open road. This buffers you from unexpected bouts of bad luck that recklessly overconfident traders don't weather.

- **Emotion Is the Kryptonite:** Skill fosters objectivity. Ego pushes overconfidence during wins and soul-crushing doubt during losses. Skill builds the calm to follow your plan even when the market acts irrationally.

Think Like a Casino, Not a Gambler

Trading success isn't about banishing luck, it's about stacking the odds:

- **Be Honest with Yourself:** Did skill create the perfect setup, or did random factors give you a boost? Self-awareness prevents hubris and prepares you for luck's eventual fickle nature.
- **One Win/Loss Means Nothing:** Zoom out! Focus on consistency and process over time. Even skilled strategies temporarily backfire; luck can reward poorly calculated risks. Don't overreact to fleeting events.
- **Humility Wins LONG Term:** Luck isn't reliable. Skills honed through analysis and disciplined execution provide your bedrock, making losses less devastating and good stretches indicators to refine, not gloat.

Conclusion

Savor victories, but never forget luck can waltz in and out

Always Striving for Improvement

That nagging feeling... are you REALLY getting better as a trader?

You know the scenario: another week of trades wraps up, some wins, maybe a few losses too. But those profits... were they from skill? Or did you just catch a lucky break? Ugh, the doubt that comes from not truly knowing can be so frustrating!

The honest truth is, there's no final "graduation day" in trading. The second you stop pushing yourself to learn and evolve, the market smells weakness and pounces. So let's break down what this quest for mastery looks like.

Why "constant growth" isn't just a trading buzzword

Here's the brutal reality:

- **Markets are wild beasts:** What worked yesterday gets shredded tomorrow. News hits, tech changes how people invest, everything shifts constantly. You gotta shift with it!
- **Your competition's on the hustle:** Other traders don't take breaks. While you chill, they're learning. Staying ahead of the pack takes work, no exceptions.
- **There's ALWAYS more to master:** New indicators, hidden patterns, ways to manage risk

even better...all this equals untapped profits. Ignoring them means leaving money on the table.

Where to focus your trader improvement efforts

Let's get specific about where improvement pays off the most:

- **Tech mastery never ends:** Don't get stale with charts and tools. New ways to spot patterns, interpret volume, and more arise all the time. Even when you're winning, stay on the cutting edge.
- **Emotions matter more than you think:** Journaling, learning to focus under pressure, coping with stress...that's how you make fewer stupid trades fueled by panic or greed.
- **Don't get stuck in one style:** Mastering scalping doesn't mean you can't learn swing trading too! New tactics offer flexibility for weird markets AND potentially more income sources.
- **Your losses are (uncomfortable) teachers:** Every bad trade holds a blueprint for what NOT to do again. Analyze them brutally, find those hidden habits dragging you down, and plug those leaks!

How to be a growth machine (not just talk about it)

Here's what traders obsessed with improvement ACTUALLY do:

- **Get comfy being uncomfortable:** The real breakthroughs happen when you push past what's easy. New setups, fixing weaknesses, admitting wrong ideas - that's how you outpace others.

- **If you don't schedule it, it ain't real:** Trading news needs time on your calendar just like live trades do. "Later" means it gets forgotten and you fall behind.
- **Find your people:** Having mentors, groups of sharp traders, etc., feeds your brain. They give you knowledge, but also keep you sharp when your solo motivation takes a hit.
- **Track your wins AND screw-ups:** It's gotta be more than feelings! Watch your win rate rise, drawdowns shrink, etc. Data keeps you motivated to grind out further improvement.

Growth in your everyday trading life

This is how it feels different...

- **After trades, ask deeper questions:** It's not just profit/loss; it's "Could I have waited longer to exit?" or "Could my entry have been tighter?" Every win gets analyzed for how to get even better next time.
- **The contrarian advantage:** When everyone's going crazy over one setup, think - who loses that profits you? Questioning the "hot" ideas opens up opportunities others miss.
- **Bored days fuel future wins:** No hot setups today? Perfect for backtesting, studying up

without market distractions, or refining how you manage risk. Those slow days make you ready to crush it when the action returns.

- **Tiny improvement habits compound massively**: 15 minutes of practice daily becomes a skill that gives an edge later on.

The bottom line (and how to fall in love with the struggle)

Steve Jobs' advice rings true in trading: don't settle for "okay." There's no mountaintop victory waiting - it's an endless process, with rewards coming as you constantly better yourself. The weird paradox is, once you truly accept and even enjoy the learning, the growth, the challenges...that's how the best traders are made.

Percentage Wisdom

"Alex began his trading journey with $500, maintaining a consistent approach. At the end of the month, he achieved a net return of $50. However, feeling dissatisfied with the seemingly small profit, Alex decided to take more risks in the next month. Unfortunately, this bold move led to significant losses instead. Alex, while evaluating his trading performance, focused solely on the absolute returns. Instead, he should have considered the percentage of returns relative to his initial capital. This oversight led him to underestimate the significance of his initial success and take unnecessary risks, resulting in avoidable losses."

When entering the world of intraday trading, it's tempting to fixate on large dollar amounts and eye-catching headlines about overnight millionaires. This narrative of "get rich quick" can be particularly discouraging if you're starting with a modest trading account. Let's shift the focus. It's time to unlock the transformative power of percentage-based thinking and reframe what it means to succeed in your trading journey.

Why Percentages are Your Best Friend

- **The Great Equalizer:** Whether you're trading with thousands or millions, markets move in percentages. A 2% increase translates the same whether you've gained $20 or $2000. Percentage-focused thinking democratizes the playing field, making account size far less significant.
- **Setting Realistic Goals:** Aiming for small, consistent percentage gains in your early trading is both feasible and empowering. Focus on making 1% days, not trying to magically multiply your account overnight. These steady wins provide invaluable capital, and, crucially, confidence as you develop your skills.
- **Power of Compounding:** Many underestimate the incredible impact of compounding, especially on a percentage basis. Let's say you steadily achieve a modest 1% daily gain. Over the course of a year, this discipline transforms your account exponentially, far outpacing strategies aimed at risky high-dollar amounts per trade.
- **Emotional Guardrails:** A focus on percentages combats the greed often amplified by large-figure aspirations. Smaller targets reduce pressure, creating mental space for calculated trades based on your chosen strategy.

Small-Account Advantage

Starting with a smaller account offers often overlooked benefits:

- **Lowered Risk:** Less at stake per trade minimizes emotional reactivity and reduces the potential for devastating losses. These early trading days are more about establishing sound habits than instant wealth.
- **Learning to Leverage Smaller Wins:** It's easier to focus on precise trade setups when striving for percentage-based wins. Instead of forcing trades or hoping for unlikely massive spikes, you master the art of optimizing trades that align with your plan.
- **Growth as a Trader, Not Just an Account:** While growing your balance is certainly a goal, your early trading journey is primarily about cultivating your skills as an astute trader. This mindset shift reduces the temptation to take rash risks when faced with a modest starting point.

Inspirational Example: Priya's Transformation

Priya began trading with a small savings account. Initially discouraged by comparing herself to those with far larger balances, she decided to focus on percentages. Starting with goals of just 0.5% daily growth, she diligently worked on optimizing her strategy. Each consistent win, though small in dollars, bolstered her confidence. Within a year, through compounding and steady discipline, Priya transformed her account to a size enabling her to move to full-time trading.

Key Takeaways

- **It's a Marathon, Not a Sprint:** Success in intraday trading isn't achieved overnight. Steady dedication to consistent percentage-based gains builds strong foundations and lasting profits far better than impulsive plays at quick riches.
- **Growth vs. Starting Point:** Don't compare your trading beginnings to another person's mid-journey. Respect the process and celebrate every percentage-based milestone toward your personal goals.
- **Psychology Matters:** A small account offers the perfect space to hone your trade execution and emotional discipline. Mastering these vital skills sets you up for long-term success regardless of what balance you eventually reach.

Conclusion

Don't allow a small account to limit your ambition as a trader. Embrace percentages as your guide, cultivate a patient mindset, and recognize your ability to achieve remarkable compounding over time. Your journey might not lead to instant fame, but through percentage-focused strategy, you will achieve genuine financial growth and, more importantly, develop the invaluable skills of a successful trader

Continuous Improvement

"Am I Better Than Last Week?" - The Question That Changes Everything

The best traders aren't always the ones with the fanciest degrees or most powerful computers. What separates them is the habit of constant self-improvement. Instead of agonizing over every tick up or down, they carve out time to ask, "What did I learn, and how does it change the way I play the game?" A weekly reflection, even a brief one, turns that into a consistent action that leads to lasting growth.

Why Bother When The Market Won't Wait?

- Stopping the Rinse and Repeat: Markets blur together easily. If you don't pause, those same costly mistakes (taking impulsive revenge trades? Ignoring stop-losses?) repeat until you burn out.
- Seeing Through the "Beginner's Luck" Trap: Everyone has a hot streak sometime. Was it genuine skill or pure chance? An honest review separates those, ensuring you build on what actually works instead of just what got you a few profitable days.
- Your Brain: The Most Underrated Trading Tool: Fear, FOMO - these control traders more than charts. Reflection makes you aware

of when your inner monologue causes bad decisions, which is the first step to reigning it in.

- Accountability That Actually Helps: It's easy to rationalize poor choices midweek. But knowing Friday you meet yourself on the page for a reality check creates a very different, much healthier form of pressure.

The Nitty-Gritty: What Does "Reflection" Look Like?

- Your Trading Confession Booth: Review your week's closed trades. No sugarcoating the bad ones or focusing only on profits. DID you stick to the plan, and where did you deviate? Why? Be brutally honest about what causes it.
- Mistakes? Yes, But Also...: What went WELL? It's tempting to gloss over the wins, but these teach you just as much! Understanding why that setup worked gives you clues on where to focus your attention in future weeks.
- Journaling Your Inner Mad Scientist: Notes you scribble while in the trenches - that fear before a big move, the boredom that made you sloppy - this kind of self-observation later reveals decision-making triggers you probably haven't even acknowledged yet.
- Plan For Next Week: Reflection without action is useless. Use this session to tweak your plan, remove losing setups, etc. You enter Monday

with a clearer game plan informed by recent events, instead of just vague hope.

Questions to Get to the Heart of Improvement

Ask yourself things like:

- Am I *truly* managing risk correctly on every trade, or am I getting sloppy when confident/overwhelmed?
- What emotion sabotaged me most this week (and what, specifically, triggered it)?
- Which patterns made the most money, and which are just traps I keep falling for?
- Where else do I NEED to get better? Don't be afraid to pinpoint weakness (chart reading, order types, etc.)

It's More Than Just Your Wallet

Go one layer deeper! Consider:

- Upgrading Your Learning: Did you make time to sharpen skills via videos, blogs, etc.? This shows real dedication to progress.
- Was I Focused, Or Simply 'Present'? A bad mood might mean even 'perfect' trades turn sour due to emotional reactions. Reflection forces you to acknowledge that, then mitigate it in the future.

In the End...

Reflecting is like checking your compass during a hike. Yeah, sometimes you discover you've wandered a bit off course...but that's how you reorient and ensure you reach your goal. It's what turns chaotic dabbling with markets into a focused journey. Even those days you have nothing spectacular to say in your log are useful if they reaffirm your commitment to stick to the process. It's time well spent because the true investment is in yourself!

Move On

Losses Suck, But Letting Them Wreck You Sucks More

We've all been there. One stupid trade tanks your gains. Doubt creeps in - is your plan garbage? Should you take a break, let the dust settle? That lingering sting from the loss hangs over you, tempting you to make bad calls from fear, frustration, or the desperate need to "win back" pride.

Here's the thing everyone tells you, but it ain't easy to actually DO: losses are part of this. The magic isn't avoiding loss, it's mastering what you do NEXT that makes you money over the long run. So how do you get that tough mindset?

Why Losses Feel Extra Crummy...And How to Hack That

Losing streaks don't just hit your wallet, they kick you in the head too:

- "Fear of Missing Out" kicks in: Those profits are gone, so you shrink back, missing opportunities. OR you bet too big recklessly to recover what was lost, digging yourself deeper. Both suck.
- Your Brain Turns Traitor: Second-guessing sets in, your own plan looks stupid now! This

freezes you when action is needed, even if your normally calm execution goes out the window.

- Revenge Trades - The Ego Trap: This isn't strategy, it's bruised pride trying to force wins. Risky moves just to get 'back to even' rarely end well. Yet we ALL fall for this now and then.
- Learning Goes Out The Window: You obsess over what went wrong, but miss the big picture lesson. Repeating losses isn't about the strategy being bad, it's usually about bad HABITS you failed to fix after the last few times they bit you!

Reset Your Brain (Yes, It's Trainable)

Top traders stay chill no matter what. It's not magic, it's rituals to shake off the past:

- Emotional Dumping: Journal your rage and frustration about the loss, THEN go re-read how well you crush it usually. Breathing exercises, physical activity - get the bad vibes OUT of your body.
- Journal is for Analysis, Not Self-Torture: What was your ENTRY bad? Sizing sloppy? Broke your own rules? Find the fixable error, don't just sit in that loser feeling.
- Markets Change, YOU Need To Too: Past winning methods don't work forever. Clinging

to old trades (good or bad) makes you blind to what's happening NOW, which likely needs a slightly different approach.

- Control Is Your Power: Obsessing over a trade you can't change is pointless. Backtest, review the plan, focus on making your NEXT trade flawless. Action beats worry!

Start Small to Rebuild Confidence

Forget ego. Small wins matter:

- Take smaller positions, find those 'sure thing' setups - it's about psychology here, even pocket change wins start dissolving the emotional impact of those losses.
- Celebrate When You Did It RIGHT: Stuck to the plan but the setup failed? That's discipline building! Over time, it's those good habits that create fat account statements.

Optimism Isn't Stupid, It's Strategic

Losing sucks, but letting it control you sucks more. Top traders use the sting as fuel:

- Proof Your Method IS Improvable: Dig into those losses, find the pattern, improve. This isn't just to feel better, it's how your next winning streak might begin!
- Short Memory = Adaptability: Each loss makes you smarter if you let it. New trade, new setups, new day. Holding onto that painful

baggage prevents the flexibility most days demand.

- The Real Battle Is Against Your Weaknesses: A few red candlesticks don't define your skill. Working though losses without losing it builds the unshakeable mindset it takes to weather the bad moments all great traders endure.

Preventing Green Days from Turning Red

"When Winning Is Your Worst Enemy"

We've all heard that saying, "Bulls make money, bears make money, pigs get slaughtered." It's a cute reminder that greed kills in the trading world. Yet, even knowing that, it's oh-so-easy to get sucked into that trap after a sweet victory.

Trading Tale: How One Good Day Went Bad

Let's say you're usually a steady trader, sticking to your system and aiming for modest gains. But one day, bam! A trade pays off way more than expected. Instead of taking those winnings and running, that little voice in your head starts whispering - maybe today's your lucky day. Time to make some *real* money.

Next thing you know, you're in a trade that isn't quite as solid as your morning win. But hey, you're on a roll, right? That trade tanks, eating up some of your profits. Now you're annoyed. Instead of quitting while ahead, you're determined to get back to where you were.

So, you jump in again - strategy takes a back seat to your gut feeling. And... that trade fails too. Just like that, your awesome gains are gone. Worse, you're tempted to do something really reckless, doubling down just to avoid ending in the red. It's the classic losing streak spiral.

The Mind Games Greed Plays

This happens because winning messed with your head. Suddenly:

- Goals Don't Matter: That first profit set a dollar amount in your mind. Anything less doesn't feel good enough, even if it's still decent money.
- Revenge Mode Activates: Now it's not about smart trading, it's about "getting those losses back." This isn't a plan, it's an emotional hijacking.
- Confidence Turns Toxic: A little confidence is essential, but a sudden influx fuels the idea that you can get away with breaking your own rules.

How to Protect Your Winnings (and Your Sanity)

It's not just about technical stuff like stop-losses. Your brain needs its own safeguards:

- Quit While Ahead: Have a daily goal, and once you hit it, consider walking away. It reinforces discipline and avoids the overconfidence trap.
- Take a Victory Lap: Step away after a big win, *literally*. Go for a walk, eat cake, do something non-trading-related. Clear your head before another move.

- Focus on Small, Consistent Wins: Chasing a massive payday breeds impatience. Small, frequent successes foster good habits, which make money long-term.

The Bottom Line

Wins are supposed to feel good! But winning can create this weird drive to make even MORE, right away. This makes you trade dumb, risking what you've built. Be happy with the profit, keep a level head, and leave greed at the door. This way, one great day doesn't ruin the whole week.

Too Big, Too Soon

You spot what looks like an incredible setup. The stars seem perfectly aligned - your chosen stock is ticking all the right boxes, ready to skyrocket. Excitement swells, and you find yourself impulsively hitting the buy button. The size of your position? Maybe three times what you've allocated on previous trades. After all, with everything pointing upwards, this feels like a sure thing.

Sound familiar? It's a tempting trap many new traders fall prey to. Unfortunately, it's almost always a path to a swift account drawdown. This chapter explores why trading too big too soon is not about bravery, but a recipe for reckless losses.

The Math Doesn't Lie

Even small losses, when applied to oversized positions, can have severe consequences. Let's illustrate:

- **Scenario 1: Cautious Trader**
    - Account Balance: $5,000
    - Risk per Trade: 1% of account ($50)
    - Loss on a trade: 5%
    - Net Loss: $25 (manageable)
- **Scenario 2: Oversized Trader**
    - Account Balance: $5,000

- Risk per Trade: 10% of account ($500)
- Loss on a trade: 5%
- Net Loss: $250 (a serious setback)

The same percentage loss generates a drastically different outcome due to position sizing.

Emotional Fallout

Oversizing doesn't just damage your account balance; it wrecks your psyche. With a massive position on, each minor pullback magnifies anxiety. Instead of focusing on chart patterns, your mind fixates on a number - how much you stand to lose right this second. This fuels two common destructive behaviors:

1. **Prematurely Closing Winners:** Fear of that loss number growing drives panic selling, cutting profit potential short.
2. **Letting Losers Run:** Instead of adhering to your stop-loss, paralysis sets in. Every tick down is excruciating, fostering the dangerous hope that "surely, it'll rebound." This often leads to far greater losses than your initial plan.

A Gradual Path to Growth

The urge to build wealth quickly is understandable. However, sustainable trading necessitates gradual risk increases aligned with proven success and an expanding account balance. It's far wiser to endure several small, manageable losses while mastering your craft than to nuke your account early on due to recklessness.

Small Wins Compound Over Time

A 5% return week after week might feel unexciting. But let that consistency compound, and within a year, you're looking at exponential growth. Oversizing positions risks derailing this long-term path for the mere illusion of an overnight fortune.

How to Right-Size Your Positions

- **Strict Risk Percentage:** Never risk more than 1-2% of your account per trade, especially when starting out.
- **Position Sizing Calculators:** Many online tools assist you with determining appropriate position size based on account balance, risk percentage, and your stop-loss level.
- **The Sleep Test:** If even imagining your current position size keeps you up at night, it's too big. Reduce it until you regain an appropriate risk/reward perspective.

Conclusion

The greatest traders embrace calculated, controlled risk-taking. Focus on consistent, small wins rather than chasing home runs; that's where lasting profitability begins. Respect the markets, respect your capital, and build confidence alongside your account balance - only then should the size of your trades increase alongside your proven abilities.

The Big Loss

Been There, Done That...And Lost Money

Okay, picture this: you think you've found the ultimate trade. Holy cow, this stock looks awesome! The indicators are flashing, the news is great, this thing is about to MOON. Your whole body gets that trading buzz, and BAM! You buy in way bigger than usual. Sure, you know those trading rules... but this is different, right?

Ugh, we've ALL been there. That rush makes even the smartest trader throw caution to the wind. Unfortunately, it's a one-way ticket to draining your account faster than you can blink. This isn't about gutsy trading, it's about setting yourself up to fail.

Math Doesn't Care About Your Hot Tip

Let's be real: even small losses hurt way more when you go overboard on a trade. Here's why:

- Small Trader: $5,000 to play with. They risk 1% on each trade (that's $50). Even if the trade flops by 5%, their total loss is only $25. Ouch, but they live to fight another day!
- Big Swing Trader: Same $5,000 account, but they buy like there's no tomorrow! Risking 10% ($500) and oops, same 5% loss. Suddenly, they're $250 in the hole with one failed trade.

See how that 'little percentage' suddenly bites hard when you bet too big?

Your Brain Goes Haywire

Losing hurts, but you know what's worse? Panic. Those big positions mess with your head! Every tiny dip on the chart feels HUGE, because that loss keeps flashing up in your brain. And that leads to two terrible habits:

- **Selling Winners Too Fast:** That little surge up a few percent looks tempting! Fear makes you snatch profit right when the trade could've actually become amazing.
- **Letting Losers Get Ugly:** Oh no, it's going down! But that loss stings so bad, you freeze. Then that little voice goes, "Maybe it'll bounce back..." It always sounds convincing in the moment, but that's how small losses get HUGE.

The Truth About Growth (It's Not Sexy)

We all want the overnight trading millionaire life. But let's be real - steady profits, one after another, that's how you *actually* get there. You gotta master the boring part first before you can handle the big wins without blowing everything you've worked so hard for.

Think Like a Math Whiz, Not a Gambler

Feeling brave? Stick to these limits:

- **The 1-2% Rule:** Especially as a newbie, this keeps losses manageable. Get into good, consistent habits now, so it's in your bones for later.
- **Calculators: Don't Do It In Your Head!** There are tons of tools online that tell you exactly how much to buy based on your balance and where you set your stop-loss. Don't guess on this, be precise!
- **Sleeping Matters:** Even if the numbers add up on paper, can you fall asleep with that amount at risk? Be honest! That little gut check saves you from terrible nights (and worse trades).

The Slow Burn Leads to Real Wealth

The greatest traders aren't gamblers, they're like super-boring athletes. Every rep has a purpose, every win builds toward their goal. You will 100% have "sure thing" setups that fail; the question is, can your account survive? That discipline early on keeps the dream alive for those inevitable monster winning streaks.

Remember, everyone feels the rush to get rich quick. It's what separates those still figuring it out from the legends - they play smarter, not harder.

The Black Swan

Those "Overnight Success" Headlines Are Lies

You see it happen – some random stock explodes 500%, everyone wants to know how they missed it. Truth is, those are like winning the lottery. Yes, someone won, but that doesn't teach you how to win next time, right? Focusing on those crazy headlines will wreck your whole trading plan.

The 'Black Swan' Trap

In trading, they call those wild, impossible-to-predict events "Black Swans". Think major crashes, new tech changing everything... that kind of stuff. It's fun to analyze *after* they happen, but trying to predict the next one? Bad idea. Here's why:

- **Leverage Makes It Worse:** People see some stock rocket up and immediately borrow tons more money to get in on the hype. Those massive wins make sense with big risks... if things go south, though, you're wiped out.
- **Risk? What Risk?** When people get that Black Swan fever, their whole plan dissolves. Stop-losses don't matter when you think you're on to the next Amazon. Then reality hits, and it's brutal.
- **Distraction City:** It takes time to become a good trader. Instead of looking at news,

studying patterns, you're glued to Twitter praying some rando announces the next market-breaking event. Spoiler alert: that's not a strategy.

Trade What You Can *Actually* Predict

The best traders? They're more like boring accountants than gamblers. They know the stock market isn't predictable, but that patterns happen all the time. That's where smart traders make their money:

- **Slow and Steady Still Wins:** Sure, a 500% overnight pop is cool, but is it realistic? Aim for those smaller, reliable wins - they snowball!
- **Treat Risk Like Your Enemy:** Always have a stop-loss, always stick to position sizing that lets you survive a few losses. This means trading what you can stomach to see go down some days.
- **Stack the Odds In Your Favor:** Does the chart setup look good? Any big news on the way for that sector? More wins come when multiple factors point your way. A hunch won't cut it.

Sometimes, "The Thing" Will Happen

Even the best traders get thrown by sudden crashes. It happens. But they do better than those "fortune teller traders" because their focus was never on those long shots. They're always playing defense, always ready for the curveball. That's how you avoid being wiped out.

Don't Miss the Forest for the Trees

Sure, it'd be awesome to guess the next moonshot, but that's not how you achieve lasting wealth. Trade what you can *know*, be responsible, and manage those losses. And hey, if that Black Swan does come flying along, maybe you'll be in a strong enough position to ride it because you played it smart until that point!

Disciplined in Life, Disciplined in Trading

The temptation to peek at charts outside market hours tugs at you, whispering sweet anxieties. That same urge strikes when a single missed workout threatens to derail your entire fitness plan. These everyday battles highlight the constant conflict between your ambitions and the alluring ease of inaction. Discipline, as they say, is truly the bridge.

Discipline - The Unseen Foundation

Technical mastery and brilliant strategy mean nothing without execution. Like an invisible current shaping the ocean, discipline fuels consistent success. Here's why your personal life habits translate directly into trading wins:

- **Emotional Mastery:** Discipline breeds resilience. A mind honed through a healthy, intentional, and structured life navigates market storms with clarity, preventing irrational trading fueled by the rollercoaster of fear and greed.
- **Habit Building:** Excellence lies in routines, not grand gestures. Just as a single salad doesn't build a champion physique, trading brilliance emerges from the daily grind of journaling, studying, and refining a plan.

- **The Transferrable Willpower:** Saying "no" gets easier with practice. Once you control cravings for unhealthy foods, for procrastination, or for mindless distractions, you build the mental muscle to cut losses as dictated by your strategy and hold winners when tempted to take profits early.

Discipline in Action for Traders

Here's how those everyday discipline victories directly empower your trades:

- **Focus Amidst Distraction:** A mind conditioned to deep, productive work (outside of trading) finds it easier to drown out market noise and distractions. That clearheaded focus enhances chart analysis and trade management.
- **Rule Adherence:** If you struggle to uphold personal goals, what makes you think you won't deviate from your stop-losses or position sizing strategies in the heat of the moment? Discipline breeds vital adherence.
- **Delayed Gratification:** Markets thrive on patience. Mastering delayed gratification in every aspect of life makes accepting the gradual rise of successful trades far easier, avoiding impulsive moves driven by fear or greed.

Discipline Combats Trading's Greatest Foes

Self-discipline becomes your secret weapon against common trading pitfalls:

- **Fear & Greed:** The disciplined trader prepares mental battle plans to handle the volatility of emotion. From scheduled chart analysis to mindfulness breathing exercises—a toolkit combats knee-jerk reactions.
- **Impatience:** Discipline teaches you to trust the process. Just as building a great physique takes consistent effort, maximizing gains (and surviving drawdowns) necessitates calculated persistence as opposed to frantic risk-taking.
- **Revenge Trading:** A disciplined life reveals quick solutions as illusions. Recovery in every arena requires deliberate action, not reckless gambles that magnify losses. Discipline makes you focus on sound strategy, not emotional vengeance.
- **Boredom-Based Blunders:** When your personal life is structured and full of meaningful activity, market analysis turns into a satisfying challenge, not a desperate search for adrenaline fueled by monotony.

Beyond the Charts - Discipline's Hidden Impact

The impact of personal discipline reaches far deeper than surface-level trade execution:

- **Clarity & Focus:** Optimal sleep, a well-fueled body, and tools like meditation boost critical thinking skills. You'll spot patterns easier, pinpoint potential pain points, and avoid errors driven by mental fog.
- **Stress Resilience:** Disciplined habits reduce your baseline stress levels. Navigating both everyday hiccups and volatile market moves becomes easier. You maintain clarity and decisive action when others succumb to panic.
- **Persistence Without Burnout:** Consistent growth is a powerful motivator. Successes outside of trading (physical fitness, learning a new skill) breed mental fortitude that helps you stick to your system through inevitable drawdowns.
- **Confidence Builder:** Small victories snowball into major momentum. Conquering challenges outside of trading strengthens self-belief. That faith makes taking calculated risks less fearful and transforms strategic inaction into decisive profit-maximizing moves.

Building the Bridge of Discipline

Turn your personal strengths into trading superpowers:

- **Transfer Success:** Where do you already display discipline? Analyze the HOW - your habits, support systems, and reward mechanisms. Replicate those strategies for trading success.

- **Audit Your Weaknesses:** Procrastination, impulsiveness, negativity—these leaks need plugging. Fix them inside and outside of trading; your charts will thank you.

- **Accountability is King:** Lean on mentors, find trade buddies, and use progress-tracking tools. We easily break promises to ourselves; support adds extra motivation when willpower fails.

- **Routine as Ritual:** Intentional structure builds self-control. From making your bed each morning to planned workouts and screen-time breaks, these habits make the necessary mundanity of chart review and record-keeping a seamless part of your day.

- **Mindfulness Masterclass:** Quiet reflection through meditation or breathwork trains your mind to stay rooted in the present moment. That focus reduces overreaction to market swings and makes it far easier to execute your pre-planned trades without distraction.

- **Visualize the Disciplined You:** Feel the weight of your ideal mental state - patient, focused, decisive. Picturing a disciplined trader's behavior cultivates those habits in moments where opportunity demands perfect execution.

Conclusion: True, lasting trading success rests upon the discipline you weave through every aspect of your life. Markets test and tempt ruthlessly, exploiting any trace of chaos within. Yet, by forging mental strength through personal routines, intentional goals, and unwavering focus, you gain an unbreakable edge that navigates market storms and delivers the victories you desire.

The Power of Specialization in Trading

Picture this: you're in a small town, they need a new doctor. So, who do you want? Mr. "I Can Do it All" (heart surgery on Tuesdays, ear infections on Wednesdays, maybe a little light chemo on the side) or dedicated specialists? Yeah, I don't want that generalist touching me either. Turns out, trading works the same way.

Specialization: The Secret to NOT Sucking at Trading

The markets are a massive, complicated beast. If you try to become an expert on every stock, every forex pair, every possible strategy...guess what? You'll end up mediocre at everything. To turn trading into something more than a hobby (read: money-losing black hole), it's about niching down and getting scary good at your chosen slice of the pie.

Choose Your Weapon (Your Trading Specialty, That Is)

Ways to go from generalist to specialist:

- **Market Mania:** Stocks, forex, options, futures... These aren't just words, they're separate universes. Pick one, learn its rules, dominate it.

- **Strategy Nerd:** Love those charts? Tech analysis could be your thing. News junkie? Maybe focus there. Find ONE style and perfect it.
- **Time is on Your Side... Or Not:** Day trading versus swing trading is like night and day. Which fits your personality AND how much you love staring at screens?
- **Sector Domination:** Become THE person everyone asks about biotech, energy stocks... whatever. Specializing means seeing those hidden gem opportunities the average trader misses.

Why Specialists Actually Win (It Ain't Just Pretty Words)

Here's the deal: when you focus, magic happens...

- **Learn at Warp Speed:** Instead of juggling a million things, you master your corner of the market fast.
- **Tools Matter:** Find the BEST indicators, communities, and news for your niche. Stop drowning in generic crap.
- **Less Stress, More Success:** Stop endlessly debating setups. Specializing means clearer decisions and less panic.

The "Okay, Fine, But How Do I Start This?" Guide

Don't stress, this isn't some overnight ultimatum. Think of it like this:

1. **Play the Field:** Demo accounts are your best friend. Dabble, find what piques your interest before risking a dime.
2. **Upgrade Your Brain:** Once you discover your thing, get obsessed. Specialist books, courses, or even finding a mentor in that area level you up fast.
3. **Fail Forward:** Nobody is perfect. Track your trades, focus on what works while ditching the rest - even within your specialty.

Forget Information Overload, It's Specialization to Domination

Markets are designed to confuse you. Specialization lets you cut through the noise. Get clear on what you trade and WHY, then the tools and the mindset start falling into place. It's about getting super strong in one area, that's how you leave the "forever beginner" phase in the dust and get on the path to actual, consistent profits.

Adapt or Perish

"Change Happens. So Adapt, or Become Extinct"

Your plan was foolproof. Then markets got volatile, some unexpected news hits, and reliable indicators are...lying to you? Frustration is natural, but what matters is how you react. Rigid trading plans get slaughtered in chaotic periods, adaptive thinkers find the new angles to exploit.

Why Change is the Only Constant in Markets

Think of markets as a living beast, it never stays the same:

- **The Big Picture Shifts:** Interest rates, the geopolitical scene...these aren't just news stories, they change how everything else behaves. Clinging to old rules during an economic swing? Recipe for disaster.
- **Tech IS the Market:** Algorithms get smarter, trading happens at warp speed... ignoring new tools or asset classes leaves you at a major disadvantage.
- **Fear/Greed Cycles Never Sleep:** When everyone suddenly panics, your calm plan means nothing if it's made for times of steady growth. The adaptable shift WITH sentiment shifts.

Rigid Traders Don't Survive, They Go Broke

If change makes you want to hide, that needs fixing urgently, here's why:

- **Dead Strategies Don't Protect You:** What worked last year (heck, last WEEK) could be obsolete. Nostalgia for past wins just means bigger losses now.
- **Opportunities Are Born In Chaos:** Everyone focused on their failing old plans won't spot that brand-new sector taking off. Those who can shift can exploit it.
- **It's Mental Warfare:** Adapt not just in what you BUY, but how you THINK as the market gets crazy. Rigidity means paralysis, a flexible mind takes calculated risks.

Adapting Isn't Guessing, It's Smart Evolution

Here's what it actually looks like to bend without breaking as a trader:

- **Never. Stop. Learning:** News, tools, deep dives into different sectors...this isn't optional, it's how to spot change before it ruins your account.
- **Backtest Like the Market Hates You:** Try your plans under every condition imaginable - crashes, rallies, sideways action. See where they hold strong, where they need modifying.

- **Take Tiny Risks to Avoid Giant Ones:** Dip a toe in a new thing, not the whole account. Learning without blowing up is the goal.
- **Don't Bet it All on One Idea:** Having diverse strategies protects you when one approach temporarily bites the dust, because markets ALWAYS keep moving.

How It Can Look in Real Life

- Trend trader suddenly stuck in a choppy market? Maybe it's time for scalping techniques instead.
- Love breakout setups? Add new volatility filters so a false surge doesn't wipe you out.
- Only play blue-chip stocks? Crypto suddenly too big to ignore, time to get educated to seize the moment.

Think Like a Trader, Not a Historian

Loving your old winning strategy is all well and good, but markets couldn't care less about your feelings. Change is how profits keep flowing, how good traders level up, and how the outdated vanish. Which trader you'll be is a choice - choose resilience, and never stagnate.

The Monday Challenge

Rishi's a familiar case. One bad Friday turns into a frustrating weekend stew of missed setups and "if only..." regrets. It's understandable...by Monday, he's itching to trade with renewed aggression. Maybe that big theory he dreamed up Saturday is the magic key? Soon, Monday turns disastrous, triggering more bad decisions in a frantic attempt to regain those lost profits.

Sound like you sometimes? Even pro traders can fall victim to the "Monday Reset" mentality. Our brains can trick us this way, especially in a fast-paced environment like trading. Let's dissect why Mondays make us go a little crazy:

The Dangers of Weekend Wishful Thinking

- **You Are NOT the Monday Market Master:** You can analyze all weekend long, but markets evolve quickly and don't care about your feelings. New info (news, etc.) pops up constantly, meaning old plans need verification, not immediate action.
- **Your Weekend Chart Brain Isn't Perfect:** Static analyses are useful, but Monday morning is live-action trading. Relying solely on past patterns without watching current setups forming in real-time is a recipe for bad surprises.

- **Revenge Trading = Self-Sabotage:** Bad endings (like Friday) stir up an "I'll show them" urge. Trading to punish the market never works out. You chase those losses with poor setups, deepening the hole you were desperately trying to escape.

How to Conquer Your Monday Trading Demons

- **Recalibrate, Don't Reinvent:** Monday morning isn't about tossing your system - it's about ensuring it's top of mind. Run through your entry/exit criteria and stop-loss rules like a mental checklist.
- **Be the Cool Observer First:** That opening bell volatility? Watch it unfold before diving in. Let initial patterns emerge - are they matching your weekend predictions, or did things shift?
- **Start Tiny Until You're Sure:** No "All In" gambles just because your ego (and last week's loss) demands it. Small, cautious trades first let you verify if Monday's market agrees with your weekend brain.
- **The Week Isn't Over After 1 Bad Day:** Trading ISN't a 5-day sprint. A measured start beats a flurry of emotionally-driven actions that set a chaotic tone for the entire week.

The Domino Effect No One Enjoys

Bad Mondays often create two types of disastrous trading weeks:

1. **Loss Avalanche:** You make an impulsive trade to recover Friday, it falls flat. Now desperation kicks in, your plan flies out the window, and losses rack up.
2. **The 'Hero' Effect:** You get lucky with ONE big risky trade early on. Boom, overconfidence kicks in, making later trades sloppy, with losses soon erasing that one 'win'.

Understanding how Mondays trigger impulsive reactions helps you build that defense mechanism against them.

In the End...

Mondays feel like a new beginning...sometimes too fresh for our own good. The illusion of resetting past disappointments makes reckless trading look tempting. Don't be fooled. Stick to your system and use Monday to observe, recenter your thinking, and ease back into your proven strategies. Your whole week (and your trader sanity) will thank you for it.

The Academic Ego

Straight-A Students Can Make Terrible Traders (Until They Do This)

"The intelligent investor is a realist who sells to optimists and buys from pessimists." - Benjamin Graham

So, here's the weird thing: the trader who was top of their class, absorbing textbook insights like a sponge, sometimes makes abysmal trades. But someone with no fancy background might somehow figure out how to consistently profit. Is trading not an "intellectual" game then? What's the missing factor?

It's not that textbook smarts don't help, but... they only get you so far. Trading requires *something else*... a set of skills no lecture hall prepares you for.

Those 'A+ Expectations' Can Set You Up to Fail

- **Pride Blinds You to Losses:** Perfect grades made other learning easy. The market offers no such kindness. You have to lose, analyze why, and grind onwards, which smarts without humility makes tougher.

- **Only One 'Right Way':** Schools reward finding the answer to a set problem. But markets constantly shift, requiring on-the-fly thinking and tweaking tried-and-true methods when they flop.

- **Too Important to be Wrong:** We get it - you were always told you're brilliant. This makes failure, especially public "bad trade" failure, excruciating. Markets will ego-check you until you learn to bounce back.
- **Thinking Instead of Doing:** Overthinking EVERY trade? Endless back-testing, but then a good opportunity zips by because you couldn't pull the trigger fast enough? Typical for high achievers.

When the 'Average Joe' Might Rise Faster

Here's what can give these guys the edge:

- **Hungry, Not Full of Themselves:** Maybe an old C in math still stings. Trading gives them a fire to prove wrong that old definition of success, focusing on results vs. bragging about being right.
- **No Idea How it 'Should' Work:** Unbound by theory, they try wild combos, sometimes discovering genius strategies the "experts" would deem too simple to work.
- **Emotionally 'Rough and Tumble':** Less focus on "being brilliant" and more on the survival instinct kicks in. Early losses aren't ego-deaths, just puzzles to solve on the way to profit.

- **Adapting as Second Nature:** They don't need a rulebook telling them things change. When their setup suddenly stops working, they move on fast, finding the *new* path to exploit.

This Doesn't Mean Book Smarts = Failure

Smart traders can excel, but...with some changes to approach:

- **Pretend Today is Day One:** All those past wins won't save you from today's losses. Stay open to new perspectives, no matter how much success you've previously seen.
- **It's the Journey, Dude:** Celebrate when you've stuck to your system perfectly, regardless of profit. This breaks the mental link between being right all the time and your self-worth.
- **Get Outside Help:** Mentors with practical, battle-tested knowledge round out your education. You get the theory down, they teach you how to apply it in the messy markets.
- **Mind Over Analysis Overload:** Quiet your constant brain chatter - trading takes decisive action too. Meditation helps manage that overthinking when those perfect setups need swift action.

Important Note: Don't write off all smart folks! Loads of super-sharp traders combine intellect with resilience, and become phenomenal.

In the End...

The market gives zero points for your degree. It cares about who adapts, gets back up after getting knocked down, and never confuses past 'wins' with a guarantee of future profits. Those traits, alongside intelligence, make the traders who win not just once, but over the long haul.

Accountability in Trading

"Accountability is the glue that binds choice and consequence." - Oprah Winfrey

Imagine a trader operating without accountability. They have a vaguely defined system, blaming losses on "bad luck" or unpredictable markets. Profits spark feelings of invincibility rather than reinforcement of solid strategy. Without honest self-assessment, improvement plateaus. Worse, mistakes can spiral into unrecoverable drawdowns.

Accountability is the bedrock of trading success. It means owning your choices, their outcomes, and using all experiences to improve your methodology. True accountability isn't a weight that crushes your spirit; it's the liberating foundation upon which skill and strategy can flourish.

Why Accountability Transforms Your Trading

- **Accelerated Learning:** Without facing mistakes head-on, you won't uncover underlying causes. Accountability speeds up the learning curve, turning setbacks into invaluable lessons.
- **Clear Progress Tracking:** Success without measurement is nebulous. Accountability involves documenting trades, decisions, and

even your mindset, charting your growth (or highlighting where you might be stagnant).

- **Enforced Discipline:** Knowing your actions are recorded provides subtle but tangible motivation to stick to your plan, preventing emotional outbursts from ruining your hard-earned progress.
- **Validated Systems:** Is your strategy sound, or have you benefited from lucky streaks? Accountability separates skill from random chance, prompting you to refine flawed approaches.

Implementing Accountability

- **The Trading Journal: Your Sacred Record:** Detail goes beyond entries/exits. Record the reasoning behind trades, your emotional state, and honest analyses of whether you adhered to your strategy.
- **Review Rituals:** Weekly or monthly sessions dedicated to finding patterns in your journal. Did overconfidence precede a string of bad trades? Do specific patterns always trip you up?
- **Accountability Partners:** Trade in isolation, and self-deception is easier. Join communities or work with a mentor. The knowledge that others have eyes on your actions promotes healthy self-discipline.

- **Emotional Check-Ins:** Trading can incite greed, fear, and regret. Pause before each trade. Is your focus clear, or are your emotions in a frenzy? Hold off until you are objectively focused.

The Mindset Shift of Accountability

Accountability isn't just numbers, it's an attitude:

- **Accept Imperfection:** You will have bad trades. Acknowledge mistakes, but don't let them define you. Shift your focus towards unearthing the 'why' behind them.

- **Ownership as Opportunity:** Each error is a chance for improvement. Analyze what went wrong, create a plan to adjust, and move forward with more refined techniques.

- **Celebrate the Wins:** Recognizing victories reinforces confidence and cements good habits, reminding you that your systems and self-discipline *can* deliver profitable results.

The Transformation

Initially, accountability might feel restrictive. Over time, it empowers you. Anxiety diminishes, replaced by clarity and strategic decision-making. You no longer feel at the mercy of the market but actively maneuver using past experiences as your invaluable tools.

The Takeaway

Accountability is a constant and conscious work in progress. Every trade, every review session, and every interaction with the trading community helps you become a stronger, more adaptive participant in the financial markets. While you cannot control market behavior, accountability puts you firmly in charge of your own trading journey.

The Comparison Game

"The only person you are destined to become is the person you decide to be." - Ralph Waldo Emerson

Picture a trader scrolling through social media. Flashy screenshots boast massive gains, exotic vacations funded by trading profits, and seemingly effortless strategies. It's easy to slip into a spiral of comparison - questioning your skills, your system, and even your worthiness as a trader.

Comparison is the thief of joy, and in trading, it's a thief of focus, clarity, and potential profits. While admiring successful traders can be a source of inspiration, letting comparison erode your confidence creates a path to self-sabotage and unnecessary risks.

Why Comparison Undermines Your Trading

- **The Unseen Struggle:** Social media is a highlight reel. You see the wins, not the countless hours of study, failed setups, and emotional hurdles overcome. Each trader's journey is unique.
- **Distorted Focus:** Focusing on others' results steals energy from improving your own strategy. You might abandon proven methods for shiny new tactics, harming your performance in the long run.

- **Breeding Impatience:** Seeing others soar fuels the misconception that trading success is instant. This sparks a chase for get-rich-quick schemes, ignoring sound risk management and the slow, steady work it takes to build competence.
- **Emotional Whiplash:** Watching others win while you struggle breeds envy. Trading on envy leads to destructive choices - revenge trades, overleveraging, or ditching your plan mid-trade out of panic and FOMO.
- **Loss of Authenticity:** Each trader has unique strengths, resources, and risk tolerances. Mimicking a style at odds with your personality is a recipe for disaster, eroding the self-knowledge crucial for consistent performance.

Cultivating an Independent Mindset

- **Your Journey, Your Timeline:** Comparing your chapter two to someone else's chapter ten breeds unfair self-criticism. Celebrate your own milestones, even small ones, acknowledging that each step contributes to your development.
- **Internal Scorecard:** Did you execute your plan flawlessly, regardless of the day's P&L? Did you handle a string of losses without emotional hijacking? True success lies in these process-oriented victories.

- **Selective Community:** Find supportive communities and mentors who challenge and inspire you without fueling competitive insecurity. Learn from others without seeking to replicate them.
- **Mindfulness Breaks:** When the spiral of comparison begins, step away. Meditation, exercise, or simply time offline recalibrates your focus, preventing harmful impulses.

The Gift of Comparison

Used correctly, comparison can be a tool:

- **Finding Motivation:** Witnessing what others achieve proves success is possible. Reframing comparison from envy to "If they can do it, so can I" channels potential, so long as your process is your primary focus.
- **Identifying Learning Gaps:** If a certain trader consistently pulls off setups you struggle with, investigate further. Are there subtle market dynamics you miss? This type of targeted analysis promotes continuous growth.

The Takeaway

Trading is ultimately a game against yourself. Each time you overcome impatience, fear, or the tempting path of imitation, you win.

Scared Capital

"It's not how much money you make, but how much money you keep, how hard it works for you, and how many generations you keep it for." - Robert Kiyosaki

"When Fear is Your Co-Pilot" - The Dangers of Trading with Scared Money

Imagine a trader whose eyes become laser beams. Not trained on charts, but their dwindling account balance. Bills loom; maybe that credit card is getting close to maxed. Each tick of the market sends an icy shiver down their spine - this isn't gambling for fun, it's a frantic escape hatch from real-world ruin.

This is the nightmare scenario of trading with "scared capital." Your financial security hangs directly on your trading success. It warps your entire process, transforming a field demanding calculated risk into a high-stakes, emotional minefield.

How Fear Sabotages Success

- **Paralysis Strikes:** Overcome by the potential consequences of failure, you hesitate. Opportunities pass you by or worse, the "do nothing" option becomes the worst, locking in losses.
- **Short-Sighted Mania:** The flip side of the coin. "Get me out of this NOW" thinking takes over. Impulsive actions and abandoning the

strategy that brought you success become the norm.

- **Risk Becomes the Enemy:** Stop-losses are ignored, revenge trading overwrites reason, positions balloon on hope rather than analysis. This isn't risk management, it's the slow-motion crash of desperation.
- **Learning Goes Out the Window:** Each loss isn't just a number. It's food off the table, a missed bill, a panicked phone call. Objectively analyzing mistakes, so critical to improvement, becomes impossible.
- **Beyond The Balance Sheet:** Trading with scared capital doesn't just ruin trades, it seeps into the rest of your life. Anxiety leads to insomnia, impacting focus. Stress makes you irritable, harming relationships. The downward spiral intensifies.

Safeguarding Your Capital, Protecting Your Strategy

- **The Truth About Tradable Funds:** Money in your trading account shouldn't be your lifeline. Its loss, while unpleasant, should not derail your life. This creates mental freedom for rational choices.
- **Start Small, Win Consistently:** Micro-positions make early errors feel almost trivial. Focus shifts from desperation to honing your

process. Only after that is proven do you slowly and thoughtfully expand your risk.

- **Build Your Fortress:** Before actively trading, shore up your overall finances. Emergency funds and steady debt reduction lower the pressure on your trading decisions.
- **Brutal Honesty:** Is that capital you set aside *truly* risk-ready, or is there a nagging worry? Listen to your gut. Better to delay than begin compromised.

This Mindset Shift Changes Everything

Trading is not a battle against fear, but a strategic waltz with it. The best traders feel fear, but they've trained themselves to use it as fuel for analysis, not rash action. Here's how to shift from panic to perspective:

- **The Long Game Mindset:** It's small, consistent wins that build lasting success, not desperate Hail Mary passes. Focus on executing your plan well, not hitting some magical number.
- **Knowledge is Your Hedge:** Before risking it all, invest time in thorough education. Paper trading, micro-trades, and backtesting help you learn on risk-free terms.

Don't Let Fear Win

Scared capital makes you fight two wars at once - one against the market, the other against your own self-preservation instincts. True trading success *can* be transformative, but only with a foundation of both clear strategy and healthy finances. Acknowledge the risk, and work to minimize its worst effects. Your future profits will thank you.

Confidence and Overconfidence

"Every man has his own courage, and is betrayed because he seeks in himself the courage of other persons." - Ralph Waldo Emerson

You know those days when everything clicks? Your timing is perfect, your reads are spot-on, and the profits flow. There's that pride, that quiet satisfaction of knowing your hard work paid off. It's tempting to keep pushing, but it's even more important to stay grounded. This is where good confidence often morphs into the destructive kind - that whispering overconfidence that can sabotage everything.

Let's be honest, sometimes it's hard to know where the line is. There's the trader who meticulously reviews their wins, analyzes what went right, and searches for areas to improve. Then there's the trader bragging on social media, swearing off all "boring" technicals, and insisting they've cracked the market with their amazing instincts. That nagging voice starts - maybe trading *is* this easy? Why not take bigger risks if that's how the big bucks are made?

Here's the trap: It's easy to become addicted to the rush of winning. Suddenly, those hard-won strategies suddenly feel too small, too safe. Dreams of mansions and lambos cloud your judgment. This is overconfidence creeping in, and it nearly always ends in disaster.

Confidence: The Steady Engine of Success

True confidence is like the foundation of a well-built house. It's built slowly, based on your experiences and proven strategy:

- **You Know Losses Can Happen (and That's Ok):** No winning streak lasts forever. Confident traders know how to bounce back and stay in the game.
- **Setbacks Are Lessons:** Losses aren't the end of the world. They're clues, pointing towards weaknesses you can fix to be an even better trader.
- **Clear Mind = Smart Trades:** A confident trader isn't ruled by panic or greed. They have the mental focus to stick to what works.

Warning Signs: When Confidence Crosses into Cockiness

- **"My Genius is Showing:"** Blaming wins on your brilliant mind while pretending a few unlucky breaks happened? That's a recipe for disaster. The market teaches humility - usually the hard way.
- **"Risk? Who Needs to Manage That?":** Overconfidence makes you arrogant. Stop-losses feel boring, taking "reasonable" profits gets mocked. Big gambles, not careful trades, are what gets celebrated.

- **Impatience = Your Enemy:** Wanting everything RIGHT NOW is overconfidence talking. Great traders know a "perfect track record" doesn't exist.

Turning Things Around: Get Confident, Ditch the Ego

- **Your Trade Journal is Reality:** Don't sugarcoat mistakes in your records. You can't fix what you refuse to acknowledge.
- **The Market Doesn't Owe You Anything:** It'll knock you down when you get high on your own hype. Staying humble prevents those nasty, costly surprises.
- **A Pinch of Doubt is Healthy:** Question your impulses before throwing money at them. Overconfidence hates questions, it only knows reckless certainty.

The Bottom Line

Being confident is powerful because it comes from self-knowledge and trust in your system. Overconfidence is all about that ego and needing "big wins" to prove your worth. The first leads to sustainable success, the other often leads to blown-up accounts. It's really that simple.

Trading Pitfalls (Especially When You're Feeling Good):

Here are some more red flags that suggest you might be tipping into overconfident territory:

- **Trading Like a Machine Gun:** Suddenly making a ton more trades than normal? Are you feeling that constant need to be 'in' on something?
- **"Who Needs Charts? It's All Vibes":** When you throw away your strategies and rely on gut feelings and hype, you've lost the plot.
- **Your Plan? What Plan?**: Not sticking to entry and exit points is a telltale sign emotions are hijacking your brain. Overconfidence hates sticking to rules.
- **My Way or the Highway:** Suddenly you know more than everyone else? Ignoring experts and dismissing the wisdom of those with more experience is a surefire way to stumble.

It's easy to slip up, even when you know better. The key is recognizing these overconfident urges for what they are and not letting them take over. Stay sharp, and most importantly, protect that trading account you've worked so hard to build!

The Event Days

"The stock market is filled with individuals who know the price of everything, but the value of nothing." - Philip Fisher

Sanjay knows his stuff. His days usually revolve around reliable setups and rock-solid stops. But then, that siren song starts...the promise of HUGE profits if he just ignores the "boring" rules for a moment. It's about to be Fed Meeting time, a total wild card! The news will drop soon, experts are making huge predictions, and several of his favorite charts look ripe for a major move. Greed starts whispering: "This is your shot at the big leagues..."

His usual discipline fades. He reasons that ignoring his event-trading ban "just this once" can't hurt. So, he breaks his own rule and dials up his positions to way larger than normal. Then the news hits...

...And nothing goes as planned. The Fed surprises everyone. The market explodes in the opposite direction, ripping through his stops like tissue paper. Panic surges, and his logical brain gets overridden by fear. He starts closing out other trades, frantically trying to "get back" what he just lost. The end result? A painful, self-inflicted wound that'll take some time to heal.

We ALL Have a Little Sanjay Inside Us

It's easy to judge when it's not your money on the line. But every trader, especially when starting out, battles that greed vs. discipline war. That news buzz, those potential monster wins... it feels like you're being left behind if you don't try and snatch at those gains. Experienced traders know that feeling is often the most dangerous one.

Big economic events are notorious for this. You know the "play safe" routine. Markets go crazy with those big announcements, prices swing wildly, and good stops vanish in a poof of digital smoke. Logic dictates taking a breather, sticking to a long-term game plan designed to minimize risk. However, it's tempting to throw all caution to the wind and try to outsmart the chaos.

Why Avoiding That Temptation is Your Superpower

- **Remember: Money Needs to Survive First:** One awful day can wipe out the gains you fought tooth and nail for. If you don't protect your account, how will you be around to trade tomorrow?
- **Discipline Breeds Discipline:** Each time you resist the impulsive "gotta trade NOW" urge, that decision makes the next one easier. It's like a mental muscle you train for consistency.
- **Learn More by Doing Less:** Watch the chaos from the sidelines and analyze why some lose

big. That detached observation teaches you invaluable lessons without risking a dime.

- **Those Opportunities Will Return:** Markets settle down eventually. Reliable patterns re-emerge, letting you strike back with much higher success odds!

Don't Wait to Become Sanjay - Plan Ahead to Resist

This isn't about shaming yourself for feeling tempted. It's about building smart safeguards *before* those tempting situations arise:

- **Calendar = Combat Buddy:** Mark all those market-shaking events in advance. Knowing when to step away removes the mental debate when the moment comes.
- **Observe, Don't Participate:** When curiosity tempts you, use delayed charts or "paper trade" (no real money!) to let the urge run its course without risking a dime.
- **Build Your Comeback Plans:** Study how markets normally react AFTER the announcement dust settles. Have potential trades lined up when it's safer to re-enter.

The Bottom Line

Don't let fear, greed, or hype trick you into self-destruction. Sometimes the smartest plays are the ones you *don't* make. When news sends the market reeling, resist the urge to join in the frenzy and watch from the sidelines instead. After the dust settles, you'll likely find far clearer trades with better setups, ready to bring back those much calmer profits.

The Anchor of Confidence

Picture the markets like a choppy ocean. One minute you're riding a wave of profits, the next you're bracing against a sudden crash. In this sea of uncertainty, confidence in your trading setup is your lifeline. But can you really hold onto that faith when losses stack up and panic whispers in your ear?

Your Setup - It's More Than Just Rules

Think of your trading setup as your personal navigational chart. It isn't just entry and exit points, it's the culmination of your research, your understanding of market patterns, and how you've decided you'll handle risk. Great traders put in serious time crafting these setups - it's a blueprint for success in this messy arena.

Test of Fire: When Losses Start Piling Up

Let's say you're Sarah, a disciplined trader. You've done the work, but some unexpected news tanks the market and your usually rock-solid plan has you on a losing streak. Doubt creeps in. Is your system broken? Do you have to toss everything out? This, right here, is when those with true confidence separate from the pack.

Trading Isn't For the Faint of Heart

Confidence doesn't mean you're blind to potential problems. It's not about ego - the best traders question themselves constantly and improve their setups. True confidence means that your faith in a well-researched plan outweighs fear during temporary struggles. You recognize that even the best strategies have bumpy stretches.

Fear - The Saboteur

It's human nature to panic when losses mount. You want to *do* something to fix it, anything! This is when impulsive trading strikes - and impulsive decision-making leads to a downward spiral of more losses. The strength is in remembering that every trader hits these patches, and those who conquer them have confidence as their shield.

How to Build (and Keep!) Trading Confidence

So, how do you get that unshakeable confidence? Here's your game plan:

- **Brutal Backtesting:** The more historical data you test your setup against, the less today's hiccups are likely to phase you.
- **Stick to the Plan:** Your rules are there for a reason. When emotions are high, fall back on the process and eliminate doubt.
- **The Long Game:** Short-term losses are noise. Focus on how well your setup has served you over months, not just this rough week.
- **Honest Reviews:** Wins and losses BOTH help you improve. Don't just obsess over losses,

break down both to find hidden strengths and tweaks.

- **Knowledge is Power:** Never stop studying the markets. Understanding why things are happening builds deeper confidence.

You Have the Power

In trading, confidence is a muscle. The more you flex it, the stronger it gets. Trusting your setup, especially when facing setbacks, prevents rash moves and ensures that when those perfect opportunities do arise, you're in the right headspace to take advantage of them. This isn't a fight about conquering the market, it's about conquering your own fear and uncertainty.

Thriving Beyond Comfort in Trading

Trading: Growth Over Comfort, or How to Avoid Stagnation

It's a fantastic feeling when everything clicks in your trading. Profits roll in, your strategies feel bulletproof, and doubt fades away. The temptation to ride this wave is real - but beware! This sense of comfort is one of the greatest threats to long-term trading success.

Why? Because markets are not your friend. They don't care that you had a good month or figured out a certain type of chart pattern. Change is the only constant. The minute you think you've "got it," you're vulnerable to surprises and stagnation. The best traders understand this; they focus on perpetual growth, not on preserving that temporary sense of mastery.

The Hidden Enemies in Your Comfort Zone

Here's why being content can eventually ruin your trading game:

- **Things Change:** News events, government policies, heck, even a single viral tweet can change market sentiment fast. Sticking to the familiar won't keep you afloat when the tide turns.
- **You're Only as Good as Your Last Trade:** Wins breed confidence, but also that sneaky "hot hand" delusion. It's tempting to assume luck is skill,

which leads to impulsive trades, ignored stop-losses, and taking unreasonable risks.

- **Strategies Fade:** Everyone notices a good setup eventually. That means what worked great last year might lose its edge - traders adapting while you rest on your laurels will pick off the profits *you* used to get.
- **Comfort is the Death of Learning:** Feeling like you've got nothing left to figure out means you're missing new patterns, opportunities, and potential flaws in your existing plan.

Mastering the Growth Mindset

This doesn't mean every trade has to be a nail-biter or that profits don't matter. It means your primary goal is constant improvement. Top traders treat losses as tuition, relentlessly analyzing what went right and wrong to make the next trade even better. Think data, not emotions.

Your Anti-Complacency Survival Kit

Here's how to make sure you never go stagnant:

- **Learn Like Your Wallet Depends on It:** News outlets, courses, trader community forums...knowledge is power. And power keeps you sharp and adaptable.
- **Mentors Matter:** Even if it's just bouncing ideas off another trader you respect, this combats the echo chamber of your own thoughts and strategies.

- **Your Journal is Your Lab:** Don't just log trades! Chart setups, news events - this lets you find patterns and tweak your methods over time.
- **Honesty Hour:** When good trades go your way, be ruthless - did your plan work perfectly, or did you get lucky?
- **Question Everything:** "Everyone" thinks the news means the price is gonna jump? Play devil's advocate - are there hidden setups if the herd moves together? This forces you to stay analytical.
- **Step Outside Your Bubble:** Maybe you specialize in stocks, but understanding how cryptos react to the same news gives you a broader market perspective. This keeps you alert.

It's a Battle Worth Fighting

Complacency whispers that this trading thing is easy, that you've hit the peak. Fight that urge. Trading successfully isn't just about the profit line, it's about outsmarting the market and pushing your own limits. Think of your brain as a muscle - if you quit lifting those heavy weights (in this case, new knowledge and hard analysis), it'll get weaker. Are you brave enough to embrace the challenge of forever adapting, to become the kind of trader who profits precisely because you refuse to stay the same?

The Masters

"If I have seen further, it is by standing on the shoulders of giants." - Isaac Newton

Embarking on a trading journey can feel like setting sail into a vast, uncharted ocean. Unexplored territory holds equal promise and potential pitfalls. However, you haven't set sail alone - countless traders have ventured into these same markets before you. Seeking out the wisdom and experience of those who have thrived in these waters can serve as your own nautical chart, guiding your course and helping you avoid treacherous trading hazards.

Why Heed the Voices of Experience

There's a unique power in learning from those who have already navigated the choppy seas of financial markets. Here's why seeking out the advice of veteran traders holds immense value:

- **Avoiding Costly Mistakes:** Every experienced trader has a catalog of "war stories" - mistakes and miscalculations made early in their journey. Their insight illuminates common errors and allows you to sidestep similar setbacks.
- **Accelerated Learning:** Markets have a way of humbling those who rush in with overconfidence. Learning from seasoned

traders compresses your learning curve. You gain access to years of accumulated insights instead of slowly acquiring them through your own trial and error.

- **Proven Strategies:** While no single trading strategy is a universal guarantee of success, studying veteran traders uncovers techniques and methods proven effective in diverse market conditions.
- **Mental Fortitude:** Trading psychology is as important as technical skill. Seeing how successful traders manage emotions, handle drawdowns, and maintain discipline becomes a masterclass in resilience.

Navigating the Sea of Information

The challenge lies in discerning valuable resources from the abundance of noise in the trading world. Where can you find those voices of experience worthy of emulating?

- **Reputable Market Analysts:** Follow recognized figures in the industry known for consistent insights, long-term track records, and a commitment to sharing knowledge.
- **Books and Articles:** Many successful traders chronicle their journeys and the development of their philosophies in books and articles. Seek out authors with demonstrated expertise and credibility.

- **Trading Communities:** Online forums and social media groups can offer insightful interactions with experienced traders. However, exercise caution: Not everyone claiming success truly possesses an authentic track record.
- **Historical Figures:** Don't overlook the timeless wisdom of legendary traders and the enduring principles they developed. Though markets change, some tenets of psychology and risk management are eternal.

The Art of Apprenticeship

While passive learning is beneficial, deeper transformation is possible by approaching veteran traders with an apprentice mindset:

- **Humility and Respect:** Approach those with demonstrable success with genuine humility and openness to learning. Avoid blind worship of any one system or individual.
- **Focused Analysis:** Study how experts frame trade setups, their risk management methods, and how they read market sentiment. This focused analysis fosters a deeper understanding than blind emulation.
- **Question and Adapt:** As with any knowledge you gain, remember to filter ideas through your own developing trading style and risk tolerance. Seek principles, not prescriptions.

Key Takeaway

The pursuit of trading success doesn't have to be a solitary endeavor. Actively seeking the insights and hard-earned knowledge of those who have traveled this path before you is akin to upgrading your boat and navigational toolkit. You set sail equipped with proven strategies, awareness of treacherous financial currents, and an understanding of the mental discipline required to stay the course. However, remember to chart your own unique course, using the lessons learned from others as valuable guideposts along the way.

Self-Reflection

"Failure Taught Me More Than Winning Ever Could"
- Basically Every Trader, Eventually

Yoda had it right. Trading failures can cut deep. All that work, and suddenly your strategy explodes in your face. The confidence built from a lucky streak evaporates faster than water in the desert, leaving behind this cold, prickly doubt. All those promises of quick fortune - lies. Trading humbles you like nothing else.

But here's the secret: those crushing moments can actually be the start of your real trading career.

Think about it: Those bad trades don't just sting, they X-ray your skills. Your ego's voice fades to a whimper, finally allowing you to see the ugly truth: where you overstretched, got cocky, or relied on luck instead of the plan. That's not failure, that's an in-your-face wake-up call, if you're honest enough to take it.

How "Setbacks" Fuel Serious Traders

- **No More Smoke and Mirrors:** Early wins? That might have been beginner's luck disguising bad habits. When those habits finally fail, you get forced to fix the root issues.
- **The Ego Takes a Backseat:** You were a hotshot on a roll...until you weren't. Losing reminds you

there's alwayyyyys more to learn. Suddenly, studying feels less optional.

- **Rethinking My Definition of 'Risk'**: Big losses shine a spotlight on whether you really knew how much you could stand to lose. Learning to handle smaller losses gracefully protects you from account-exploding ones later.
- **Emotions 101 (for Real This Time)**: Was it your awesome plan, or that jolt of fear, making you hit the buy button? Setbacks expose the gap between good strategies and letting your feelings run the show.

The Comeback Begins...Here's How

- **Back to the Drawing Board**: Remember those basic things you skipped at the start? Turns out complexity isn't a shortcut to profit. Master the simple building blocks for stronger performance.
- **Mini-Me Trades**: Scaling your positions waaaay down lowers the emotional heat. This lets you practice sticking to the plan without panic setting in.
- **My Journal & Me, Ugly Truths Included**: Don't just log what went wrong, but those feelings before the bad trade - overconfidence, boredom, etc. That makes it less likely you'll make the same mistake next time.

- **Find Your "Been There" Tribe:** Turns out everyone's face-planted at some point. Chatting with those who clawed their way back up is super motivating.

The Trader You Become When You Refuse to Quit

Losing trades can reforge you, but only if you let them:

- **No Fighting the Market, Understanding It:** You were trying to conquer it, now you aim to coexist with its crazy ebbs and flows. Losses teach this harsh, essential lesson.
- **Honesty = My Growth Engine:** Blaming bad luck gets you nowhere. Admitting the mistakes you DID make puts you back in control and able to improve.
- **Focus is EVERYTHING:** Your success now boils down to: a well-built plan, controlled emotions, and the drive to get better every day. This creates the consistency winners are made of.

In The End...

The most devastating "failures" in trading are the ones that drive you away from the market for good. Those humbling moments - those are the turning points if you take them as fuel for improvement and rebuild from a smarter place. Don't get discouraged, because those losses were a painful investment in your trading education. It's part of the path to becoming a trader who not only survives but thrives.

Full-Time Trading?

Is Full-Time Trading Your True Calling?

The dream is powerful: no boss, no commute, making big money from the comfort of home. No wonder everyone thinks they should ditch a cubicle job and go full-time trader! But hold up. That Instagram hustle-culture hype paints a pretty picture, but the reality is less glamorous and way more risky.

First, Know What You're Risking

You gotta ask yourself these big questions. And be honest - lying to yourself ruins everything:

- **Money Matters:** Do you *really* know how much it takes to live comfortably each month? Don't focus on big wins. Will steady trading consistently cover the everyday stuff?
- **Stress Test:** Trading isn't about luck, it's about handling loss like a pro. Can you stomach seeing your account get chopped down without panicking and making dumb moves?
- **Trading, Not Investing:** Day trading requires active attention, making quick decisions. It's a world away from those buy-and-hold investment plays. Do you have that skillset?

Don't Leap Until You've Proven...

It's more than just having a system. Before full-time trading even makes sense, you need:

- **Cash Reserve:** A big enough emergency fund means losing trades won't make you lose your house. That level of pressure breaks even the best traders.
- **Long-Term Wins:** Everyone gets lucky sometimes. Can your strategy bring small, consistent profits over many months, through different market moods?
- **Unbreakable Focus:** No boss means no one but YOU keeps you on track. Do you thrive with absolute freedom? Most people don't, at least not at first.

Think Like You've Already Quit

The switch to full-time trading changes everything, especially inside your head:

- **Your Own Worst Enemy:** Suddenly, losing streaks mean not just less money, but the inability to pay your bills. This triggers emotional trading, and that ruins you fast.
- ***Are You a Loner?*** Trading is isolating. Missing the office chit-chat might sound great initially, but that support system matters more than you realize.
- **Taking The Blame:** When something goes wrong, it's all on you. That requires a special

kind of resilience to face failures and get better, not bitter.

One Last Thought

Making it as a full-time trader is the real win. The ability to do that comes from carefully understanding the true risks AND knowing yourself well enough to know if you can handle those risks. Don't blindly chase a dream you're not built for. Instead, start small and grow steadily as you prove you have what it takes. That's way smarter than burning out early because your expectations didn't match reality.

Beyond Monetary Pursuits in Trading

The person who starts simply with the idea of getting rich won't succeed; you must have a larger ambition." - John D. Rockefeller

Rockefeller wasn't wrong, chasing quick bucks alone leads to ruin. True trading fulfillment requires seeing that profits are the means, not the ultimate ends. Think of trading less as a money grab, and more as a demanding (yet immensely satisfying) personal development program, with incredible financial upsides.

Imagine you gain that deeper insight: suddenly, it's not only about trade results, but the type of person you become along the way.

Intellectual Stimulation: Your Brains Ultimate Workout

Markets never get boring. Think of them as ever-shifting puzzles influenced by world events, psychology, and complex economics. To stay ahead, you learn, adapt, and outsmart constantly:

- Critical Thinking Upgrade: Your ability to find reliable patterns, question news hype, and spot flawed setups sharpens in ways no desk job ever could.
- News Becomes Meaningful: The world suddenly makes more sense. Those dry economic

releases? Those reveal potential trading gold hidden in plain sight.

- Perpetual Learning Cycle: No stagnation here. New strategies, technologies, and changing market dynamics keep you intellectually challenged and mentally vibrant.

Personal Growth: Trading Fortifies More Than Just Your Portfolio

Trading strips you bare emotionally. This painful process builds a resilience and internal clarity few will ever achieve:

- Emotions Become Tools, Not Tyrants: Fear, greed, impulse...these lose their grip when discipline reigns. This mastery transforms not just trades, but ALL life decisions.
- Losses Teach What Success Never Could: Losing streaks teach patience, thoroughness, and focus on process - none of which come easily by winning blindly.
- Accountability = True Power: Blaming forces outside your control keeps you powerless. Trading demands you confront errors to fix them, unlocking genuine agency.

Community & Mentorship: Trading as a Collaborative Endeavor

While solo execution is required, finding 'your tribe' becomes a catalyst for faster growth:

- Combat Loneliness, Strengthen resolve: Surrounding yourself with like-minded traders keeps you sane, holds you accountable, and lets you experience camaraderie even in isolated work.
- Shared Genius: Forums, study groups, or a strong mentor accelerate your learning curve exponentially. It's the difference between solo trial and error versus having seasoned guides.
- Pay It Forward: Once your footing is stronger, helping newer traders forces you to solidify your own knowledge. Teaching IS learning, and builds community you rarely find outside of trading.

Trading: Empowering a Life You Truly Want

The most successful traders understand profits unlock potential far beyond luxury buys:

- Freedom as the True Commodity: No 9-5 grind, location dependence, or answering to an uninspiring boss dictates your path. You own your time.
- Building Something Deeper: Whether it's generational wealth, a life of giving back, or funding the passion project of your dreams,

markets grant you the means to do more with your one life.

- Life On YOUR Terms: Imagine designing your day around what fulfills and nourishes you. Energy peaks mid-morning? That's trade time. Trading lets you escape the "one size fits all" limitations of traditional work.

Focus on the Journey, Not Just the Destination

The money obsession leads to burnout, bad decisions, and ultimately, lost profits. Traders wise enough to seek something greater within the process itself enjoy an additional edge:

- Challenge Becomes Its Own Reward: The market puzzle, the personal growth...this hooks you more than any single winning month ever could. This breeds longevity.
- Losses Hold Their Own Wisdom: When the "trader you become" outweighs the immediate balance sheet, drawdowns hold less sting and fuel a desire to grow stronger.
- Sustainable Mindset: It's an unending, exciting path of ups AND downs. This perspective lets you weather both with calm confidence, avoiding the self-destructive swings less resilient traders succumb to.

The Secret of Long-Term Success

Ultimately, the traders who love the game far beyond the promise of instant wealth thrive. It's in that space where market expertise fuses with personal transformation. The profits then become a natural byproduct of this rich, evolving, and endlessly interesting pursuit. Trading then becomes one aspect of a truly impactful life, not the source of your entire identity.

www.ingramcontent.com/pod-product-compliance
Lightning Source LLC
LaVergne TN
LVHW100314210926
848480LV00003B/1120
* 9 7 9 8 8 9 2 7 7 5 0 8 3 *